MARC BOLAN

BEAUTIFUL DREAMER

JOHN BRAMLEY

MUSIC
PRESS

Published by Music Press Books
an imprint of John Blake Publishing Ltd
3 Bramber Court, 2 Bramber Road,
London W14 9PB, England

www.johnblakebooks.com

www.facebook.com/johnblakebooks 🅵
twitter.com/jblakebooks 🆃

First published in hardback in 2017

ISBN: 978 1 78606 448 6

British Library Cataloguing-in-Publication Data:

A catalogue record for this book is available from the British Library.

Design by www.envydesign.co.uk

Printed in Great Britain by CPI Group (UK) Ltd

1 3 5 7 9 10 8 6 4 2

Papers used by John Blake Publishing are natural, recyclable products made from
wood grown in sustainable forests. The manufacturing processes conform to the
environmental regulations of the country of origin.

Every attempt has been made to contact the relevant copyright-holders, but some
were unobtainable. We would be grateful if the appropriate people could contact
us.

John Blake Publishing is an imprint of Bonnier Publishing
www.bonnierpublishing.com

'The individual has always had to struggle to keep from being overwhelmed by the tribe. If you try it, you will be lonely often, and sometimes frightened. But no price is too high to pay for the privilege of owning yourself.'

FRIEDRICH NIETZSCHE

AUTHOR'S NOTE

Many of the contemporary reviews and articles on Bolan's work which are referred to in this book came from clippings in my personal scrapbooks. Like many teenagers, when I cut out anything of interest on Marc Bolan, I rarely had the foresight to include the date or the writer! Whilst the vast majority of these publications are now defunct, I apologise for the occasions on which I have omitted reviewer bylines while putting *Beautiful Dreamer* together.

CONTENTS

HEREIN LIES THE BELETH DEER

All silken hide and silver clear,
Antlers bound with taloned gold.
Men are young, the stag is old,
In coldest morn or summer's heat
Are ever heard its stalking feet.
Hoof to bough and bough to sky,
Nothing escapes that ancient eye.
In forest lost from mortal Ken
Where Gods debate the ways of men,
A silver streak, a golden gleam
Of the beleth deer, great kings do dream.

From the published 2015 collection of poetry,
Marc Bolan – Natural Born Poet

PREFACE

'I don't know why we need to make a record. All we need to do is
put up posters all over town and I'll be just as big a star.'
MARC BOLAN

Four decades have now passed since the untimely demise
of Mark Feld, a.k.a. Marc Bolan, in a car crash on the
morning of 16 September 1977. During that time, a great
number of biographies of this singular star have been published.
Authors who had no affinity with Bolan have written well-
researched tomes about him. Some of the people who worked
with him have chipped in with their own biographies; certain
passages in these, I would suggest, have been unworthy of
Bolan's memory, not to mention unworthy of those who wrote
them. Last and by no means least are those books written by
people who have been Bolan fans for ever; these books should
be appreciated if for no other reason than they represent a
genuine fan's connection with the singer.

When the opportunity presented itself in 1991 to write about
my all-time music hero, I could not resist. *The Legendary Years*

was a fan's hastily put-together appreciation of Bolan's life, including a collection of stunning pictures, hitherto unpublished.

While the working-class hero of my generation was (and remains) John Lennon for charisma, persona, mysticism – only Marc Bolan gave me everything that I desired as a teenager, riding white swans into worlds uncomplicated by reality, through songs and poetry. Along with millions of other fans, I was enchanted by 'The swan king, the Elf lord, the eater of souls', entered willingly into the heavily Tolkien-influenced mythical world of Rarn – a fantasy world that constantly drifted in and out of the consciousness of Bolan in all his guises: the Motivator, Teenage Dreamer, Electric Warrior and the Dandy in the Underworld. Even now I still revisit the worlds created by him with as much enjoyment as I did all those years ago.

My publisher, John Blake, and I agreed that *Beautiful Dreamer* should be a time capsule of nothing but happy Bolan memories, free of salacious hearsay. Written by a genuine fan, for genuine fans, with input from genuine fans. Now *that* is a challenge worth accepting, and I did so without hesitation. Marc Bolan was a beautiful man with a talent those who followed him could only aspire to. I wanted to shine a light on what he was, to look at the beautiful visions that he revealed to us, the fans.

For this project, I decided to set aside everything that I had written about the years my wife Shan and I – seemingly single-handedly at times, with little help from within the music industry – strove to find new and inventive ways of keeping the name of Marc Bolan on people's minds. Of course, we were aided in no short measure by those wonderful fans who vowed never to forget Marc, and who followed him devoutly, as we did in the 1960s and 1970s, along with those who were new to the Bolan phenomenon.

So much had been written about Marc Bolan that (while researching was, at times, a rather difficult task due to the sheer volume of words), the more I read, the more enthralled I became. All I have ever really known was Bolan the artist. I am indebted to all those who gave us the opportunity to read his own words, as they are the essence of who he was. Yes, he was a poet, songwriter musician and entertainer. He was also, however, a dreamer. He had a head full of images, words, music that screamed to be exposed. Whether Marc said something in 1965, 1975 or 1971 is immaterial: his words are beautifully ageless.

One dictionary definition of glam rock runs, 'A style of rock music first popular in the early 1970s, characterised by male performers wearing exaggeratedly flamboyant clothes and make-up.' I have always believed that glam rock started way before the 1970s. Yet, for me, glam rock – with or without the lipstick – was reinvented when Marc Bolan shook his head full of curls and turned his face into the camera on the BBC's *Top of the Pops*. Yes, he was a good-looking young man, but he was aided by the chance shimmering of light that crossed his face, revealing glitter on his cheeks. It was to be an awesome period of music in an otherwise dreadful, uncertain Britain that faced many sociological challenges and seemingly had no answers.

To understand the historical context of the sixties and seventies, in which Marc Bolan excelled, it is worthwhile in my opinion reflecting upon a little social history. In the first fifty-three years of the twentieth century, there were two major conflicts that gripped Britain, not to mention the rest of the world. The mass destruction of both humanity and infrastructure that began with the First World War claimed over 8 million casualties – military and civilian – on both sides combined. Following two decades later, the Second World War claimed in total more than 21 million military lives and more than 27 million civilians. Despite the mass mechanised slaughter, Britain still managed to record a population of some 50 million by 1952. Little wonder that, come the midway point of the fifties, Britain and the world in general was weary of war and destruction.

All the nation wanted was an end to their torrid period of history. There was some good news emerging: tea, sugar and meat rationing ceased; employees started to receive company pensions and work practices and regulations began to improve, although there was still a long way to go; the average wage in the decade was in the region of £10 a week; consumer goods were introduced in the form of electric fires, cookers, vacuum cleaners and washing machines. Somewhere in the region of 15 per cent of consumers had a fridge and a mere 10 per cent could communicate using a home telephone. The shopping was in general a daily chore for most, as you could expect to take most of a day popping into the greengrocer's, the butcher's and the fishmonger's.

Britain still held onto the merits of keeping the death penalty. The hanging of Derek Bentley in 1953 caused a huge debate as to the merits of such methods of punishment before his posthumous pardon in 1993. It was of no use to Ruth Ellis: she was the last woman to be executed in the UK in 1955. Hanging shamefully remained a punishment in law until the mid-sixties. Homosexuality was not just frowned upon: if caught engaging in homosexual acts, a gay man would be arrested and, in most cases, a lengthy spell in prison ensued. In the same decade, gangs of Teddy Boys roved the streets of London, looking for black people and other minorities – mixed-race couples in particular – to attack. The unrest, of course, guaranteed exposure on newspaper front pages. This led successive governments to limit immigration and to attempt, in a half-hearted fashion, to quell racist attitudes against people who had already settled in Britain. Social morals were conservative, attitudes far from progressive, and London was a grey capital, lacking the buzz and vibrant cosmopolitanism it possesses today.

Yet in this dour period the world would change for ever when Elvis Presley arrived at Sun Records in Nashville, Tennessee, to give birth to rock music as we know it today. He was to dominate the charts and become the first artist to inspire mass hysteria among young girls and older women alike. Of course, rock 'n' roll was not simply about Elvis, but he took centre stage, with help from a few friends. The years that followed produced many similar 'boy next door' artists. Elvis Presley, of course, was the ultimate icon. His voice, hand in glove with his good looks, guaranteed that he would be treated with reverence; and those who followed him – Cliff Richard, Tom Jones, Tommy Steele, Adam Faith – all owed a debt to him.

If the nineteen fifties were in sepia, then the sixties were transformed into a Technicolor wonderland, in the aftermath of this rock-and-roll explosion. The decade became known as the Swinging Sixties. It heralded what was to be a defining decade for Britain. The capital city was at the forefront of a transition from grey into a shining metropolis of the world, full of freedom, hope and promise.

The decade started well with the emergence of the first of the super groups, the Beatles, when they debuted at the Cavern club in Liverpool, launching a career that was to span ten years, yet be revered nearly sixty years later. The Rolling Stones, Jimi Hendrix, Cream and Pink Floyd were just the tip of the iceberg of rich musical talent that emerged to drive music forward and give the youth of an otherwise stuffy society a voice, a purpose and the confidence to want to be individuals. This musical wonderland was to have a massive effect on fashion and the perception of what boys and girls should look like.

It was a slow evolution rather than a dramatic revolution. Quietly at first, another genre emerged, that of the hippy movement. Inducing a spirit of free thought, free love and peace rather than war, the hippy movement started to gather pace – and it is at this juncture that Marc Bolan was to emerge, after a few false starts. For young Marc would fall into line with this newfound optimism and desire to be an individual, to be different. It is little wonder, therefore, that Marc dreamed and created as he did.

For those of you who may have only a slight understanding of what all the fuss is about, or for those new fans with only limited understanding of Marc Bolan and his music, I hope the following will whet your appetite to want to learn more about the Beautiful Dreamer. At the end of the book, I have listed suggestions that will, I hope, enhance your enjoyment of this iconic singer and his work. For those of you who know it all off by heart: you have my utmost respect and I hope you will be able to forgive me for going over it all yet again!

PART ONE

THE THRONE
OF TIME

FRIDAY, 21st NOVEMBER at 7.45 p.m.
Tickets: 15/-   12/6   10/6   7/6

from Hime and Addison, 37 John Dalton Street, Phone: BLA 8019, and Lewis's.

Roy Guest and Vic Lewis present

for the lion
and the unicorn
in
the oak forest
of faun

Tyrannosaurus
Rex

in concert with
John
Peel
and friends

A
HEMS
PRESENTATION

HIP
GNO
SIS

DEWELLA

A mansion forged on foundations of fire,
A wallet of indigo and pitchfork of Amelian gold
Were the dying gifts to me from the Bird-man of Arcadia,
Once sky-lord in the Halls of Pan.

The diamond domed courts
Marbled and green
Have long since been ruinous home
Of the mountain goat and winter's boys,
Simple and starless,
Wanderers of the moors forever seeking wisdom
In the guise of Dewella,
Goddess of The Pathways and Wooded Dells,
Daughter of the great Ganatik river.

Fluid and silver,
Upon the swans of green she has been seen at midnight
Slaughtering shadows with her trident.

For all that is Summer-born hateth The Shadow Clans
And she at her birth held a fiery comet in her teeth
And laughed at The Maker of The Universe.

From the published 2015 collection of poetry,
Marc Bolan – Natural Born Poet

1947–69

'I'm just a rock-'n'-roll poet who is bopping around on the side'
MARC BOLAN

Mark Feld was born into a working-class Jewish family on 30 September 1947 in Hackney General Hospital, east London. He had one elder brother, Harry, though they had little in common. Harry was a heavy-set, generally quiet boy who seemingly took after his father in persona but his mother in physical attributes. Mark Feld was quite a different matter. In an interview with me in 1991, June Feld, Marc's widow, revealed that having met Marc, and then his family, she found it difficult to believe that they were genetically related: 'They were just a normal-looking family, whereas Marc was an extremely beautiful man that every girl would dream about.'

That said, the young Mark Feld clearly mirrored the forceful, no-nonsense exuberance and welcoming nature of his mother. In 1975, talking about his early life, he would make audacious claims about his childhood memories. 'I can remember sitting up in my pram, shaking a rattle,' he told rock journalist George Tremlett, adding, 'I can remember sitting under a table in the kitchen [. . .] looking up women's skirts' Marc added, proudly. 'I must have been a healthy four-year-old.'

His penchant for saying whatever came into his head never left him. June would often reflect that Marc was incapable of being straightforward. 'He was as complex as he was simple in outlook,' she told me, with a smile, looking back on those early days. 'By that, I mean that he never really bothered to think through what he was saying. To him, it did not matter, because in his own head it was relevant, it was true in his eyes.'

His early education was, in Bolan's own words, a 'bore'; he had little interest in the mainstream subjects we all have to learn. He passed from Hackney's Northwold Primary and William Wordsworth Secondary Modern School, his final educational destination being Hillcroft School in Wimbledon. He was far from content there. 'In the end, they expelled me,' Marc revealed. in one interview (quoted in the online *Unzipping the Abstract*). 'They were very nice about it. They really didn't seem to mind at all and as I only had another six months to go before my fifteenth birthday when I could leave school anyway. [. . .] I think the teachers breathed a sigh of relief. They considered me to be a bit eccentric.' He went on to complain, 'They just wouldn't answer my questions at school. I mean questions about real-life things, about the whole business of growing up.' He continued, 'I wasn't being taught anything I wanted to learn about . . . while the rest of the English class wrote essays on Wordsworth, I was writing my own short stories about Norse gods.'

'I wasn't a spoilt child,' he emphasised to the *Evening Standard*'s Maureen Cleave in late 1965. 'All I did was tell my mother what was best.'

'I was a weird kid, very fucked-up as a kid,' Bolan told journalist Keith Altham in 1972.

June Feld surmised that, emotionally, Marc endured many different experiences while growing up: 'He was fortunate to come from a solid family background. Marc never really got too involved with anyone and never formed friendships. He really didn't think that friendships mattered.'

Indeed, Marc himself recalled, 'I used to read a lot and I was very into gangs, not fighting gangs. I was always, like, the leader of all the things I ever did, but very solitary. I was always a centre for envy of some sort, only I never understood why.

Amid all the chaos surrounding his education, Mark Feld woke up to the contemporary mod scene. This 'scene' had evolved as an extension of the fifties beatniks and centred on modern jazz and philosophy, amphetamines and blues artists such as John Lee Hooker. He appeared in a large glossy magazine, *Town*, as part of a pictorial feature on mod fashions. *Town* was a serious publication, one that anticipated men's style magazines such as *GQ* and *FHM*. Its September 1962 issue featured an article by Peter Barnsley about mods, under the heading 'Faces Without Shadows' – apparently a reference to the youthful faces who were at the forefront of the new scene. The photographs were taken by Don McCullin, now recognised as a distinguished war photographer, and are acknowledged as the first photographs of the future star to appear in print. The piece offers an interesting insight into the then undiscovered Mark Feld: 'Feld is fifteen years old, and still at school. [. . .] The queues of Teds outside the cinemas in Wimbledon look just like a contest for the worst haircut, he says. At least the boys of Stamford Hill dress sharply, and who would want a new, clean house if it is in unsympathetic surroundings? [. . .] Where is the goal towards which he is obviously running as fast as his impeccably shod feet can carry him? It is nowhere.'

Feld boasts to Barnsley, 'I've got ten suits, eight sports jackets, fifteen pairs of slacks, thirty to thirty-five good shirts, about twenty jumpers, three leather jackets, two suede jackets, five or six pairs of shoes and thirty exceptionally good ties.' Marc states this with a panache that was to be one of his hallmarks throughout his career. He adds, 'Three years ago [. . .] we used to go around on scooters in Levi's and leather jackets.' Barnsley comments, 'But you would have been twelve years old!' 'That's right,' responds the precocious, smiling teenager.

In August 1967, the *Observer* colour supplement examined the mod trend. Marc was featured again – although by this time, as a nineteen-year-old, he had moved on and was working in the music business himself as Tyrannosaurus Rex. 'I thought those mods were just fantastic. I used to go home and literally pray to become a mod,' he enthused. Oddly, however, just three years later in an interview for the British publication *ZigZag*, he said of that period, 'I found that clothes thing very appealing visually, and I got right in there and made myself look like these other cats, who were somewhat older than I was. By the time the mod thing really happened, I was out of it and living in France.' In a somewhat surreal interview in 1972 with Michael Wale for the magazine *Vox Box*, Marc expanded on the theme of being a mod:

Well, I was at the forefront of that movement. I was still at school and used to steal scooters, which was one of my great hobbies. I got busted once, that was very naughty, used to chrome the bubbles. What turned me on about that period was the total involvement materially with what was going on, because it was a complete involvement with perhaps seven people that one respected and really being important to be the leader of that materially. It was very material, down to clothes, totally. The only places I used to get clothes from was Vince's and Domino Male and these sorts of places in Carnaby Street.

[. . .] I used to go in there because I dug the clothes. There were no mods as such, just people. I used to have my shoes made. We had four or five people that supplied what you wanted and occasionally one would get other clothes like Levi's. [. . .] there was a place in Leman Street, Whitechapel, which used to have them . . . All the clothes were Army surplus and this was a sort of surplus store and we just pulled up there on literally 40 scooters. And there was a big pile of Levi's and we just stole the lot. [. . .] one wanted them and one took them. My scooter had zipped off without me and I stuck the Levi's up my jumper and I ran down the road and got a bus. My heart was pounding away. It was great knowing we were only one of a few people in England who had them.'

At this point it would be fair to state that Marc had no clear vision of where he wanted eventually to emerge, in both life and in his career. He picked up some bit parts as a walk-on extra, for the children's TV show *Orlando*, among others. He was later to claim that he made far more television appearances, but they have not surfaced to date and therefore his claim must remain unsubstantiated. Musically during this period of uncertainty, he decided to promote himself as a folk singer, taking the name Toby Tyler. With only his guitar for company, he had no one else with whom to forge any kind of musical partnership.

It was during this period that the first of his many managers recognised his potential. Allan Warren was born in Wimbledon on 26 October 1948. He went on to become a high-society photographer, but started out as an actor, known initially for the film *Here We Go Round the Mulberry Bush* (released in 1968), and subsequently appearing in *Queen of the Blues* and *Porridge* (both from 1979). Warren was later to remark that he saw in Marc a 'baby-faced Cliff Richard'. The two formed an agreement – couched in the loose terms characteristic of the naïveté of the 1960s – declaring that, should Toby Tyler become successful, Warren would manage his affairs. Marc did a recording test for Decca singing the Betty Everett song 'You're No Good', but failed to impress. Not surprisingly, the fledgling relationship was terminated soon afterwards and Marc cast aside the name Toby Tyler.

Fate, as they say, favours the brave, and sheer doggedness and determination to succeed led Marc to search out the enigmatic Phil Solomon in London. Solomon managed some of the 1960s' biggest acts, having discovered the likes of the Bachelors and the solo female artist Twinkle, the latter having enjoyed a major hit with 'Terry' (a song the BBC banned because its subject matter – the death of the eponymous hero in a motorcycle crash – was considered morbid). Solomon later became a key mover and shareholder in Radio Caroline, a station that anyone who grew up in the 1960s will remember and may well have tuned in to. It was by this time banned from transmitting on the mainland, and so had moved offshore – very successfully.

The approach to Solomon started a chain reaction that was to introduce Marc to Mike Pruskin, a PR man with connections that included (ironically) the Decca Records producer Jim Economides, who had previously shunned Marc in his guise as Toby Tyler. This time, the collaboration led to Marc's being introduced to, and then signing with, Decca. Within a short time, he found himself in the company's studios, working with Economides and musical director Mike Leander. The 10 September 1965 issue of *NME* announced that Decca had signed '17-year-old folk singer Marc Bolan from London. Songs by Burt Bacharach and Sonny Bono (of Sonny and Cher fame) are being considered for Marc's first disc which will probably be issued around mid-October.' The tracks that made up the A- and B-sides of his debut single were 'The Wizard' (several years later, this track resurfaced as a stunning re-recording on the excellent 1970 *T. Rex* album of the same name) backed with 'Beyond the Risin' Sun'; both were self-compositions.

The single was released on 19 November 1965 and early signs were good. Reviews likened Marc to the English poet and novelist Walter de la Mare, as well as comparing his voice to that of Sony Bono. As for 'The Wizard', *NME* columnist Derek Johnson noted in the issue of Friday, 26 November, that the track 'has a most intriguing lyric' and added that the singer was 'offset by a solid thumping beat, strings and ethereal voices'. Another – unnamed – reviewer wrote, 'On the strength of this strange young man's looks and weird background I suspect we'll hear more of this odd record about meeting a wizard in the woods who knew all.'

Marc appeared on several music TV programmes, including the Rediffusion *Five O'Clock Funfair* at teatime on Tuesday, 23 November. He appeared alongside acts such as the Walker Brothers, the Bachelors, Paul and Barry Ryan and the Searchers on *Thank Your Lucky Stars*, screened on 18 December 1965.

The year ended with the singer once more in the Decca studios – but no one was sufficiently inspired by the tracks he recorded to want to release them. Leander parted company with Marc and it was left to Economides to put an arm around the singer and push him to write more material. Marc put 'The Third Degree' before his producer and studio time was booked. Out of necessity, with Leander gone, a new sound now emerged. On release, one unnamed reviewer suggested that 'The Third Degree' was 'the best yet from the singer songwriter. More powerful, well-worded, fastish tempo and all-in backing sounds. Given plugs should do very well.' The single was certainly a progressive move away from the ambience of 'The Wizard': the mellow orchestra and vocal backing (by the Ladybirds) on his previous single was now replaced with a band that delivered what was described as a 'contagious driving shake beat keeps you moving to the rhythm, as Marc Bolan dual-tracks this swinger'. Despite the heady momentum that was gathering, thanks largely to the Pruskin management/publicity machine and the charisma and self-assurance of the singer himself, neither of his first two singles enticed the public to buy into the dream. Unfazed, Pruskin contacted Simon Napier-Bell, who had written and produced the No. 1 single 'You Don't Have to Say You Love Me' for Dusty Springfield and who was then managing the Yardbirds. Napier-Bell turned down the opportunity to produce Marc, owing to his other commitments, but that was not to be the end of the story.

Bolan, now without Pruskin to assist him, decided once more to approach the in-demand Napier-Bell. 'Somehow, he got hold of my home telephone number and simply called me up,' Napier-Bell later revealed. 'I'm a singer and I am going to be the biggest rock star ever, so I need a good manager.' Simon responded by suggesting that Marc should send a tape to his office. With a great deal of nerve, not to mention confidence (which the singer could never be accused of lacking), he told Napier-Bell that, as he was quite close to his house, he could drop in with the tape.

A short while later, there was Marc on Simon's doorstep, with a huge smile on his face and a guitar around his neck. A personal appearance by an aspiring musician was usually the thing that Napier-Bell hated most: there was nothing worse than listening to someone without knowing how or when to stop them. But he let Marc right into his home, having seen instant evidence of his panache and star quality. Marc sang to him for about fifty minutes and in the end the manager stopped him – not because he hated what he heard, but simply because he wanted to call a studio and book a session.

At eight o'clock that evening, Marc started his performance again. Listening to the tapes the following day, Napier-Bell thought he sounded even better and was convinced that one of the recorded songs could be a hit single. 'Hippy Gumbo' was produced by Napier-Bell and included a string section. The single was reviewed by one music paper as 'a crazed mixture of an incredibly bad female Negro blues singer and Larry the Lamb'. Another review was far more enthusiastic – showing the diversity of opinion that Marc has always aroused: 'This one could easily make it because of the unusual, tense, dramatic voice used this time by Marc, sort of wavering . . . like an old jazz singer.' The single failed to enter the charts.

Next, Napier-Bell suggested that Marc should join another of his bands – John's Children. Reportedly, the manager decided to place Marc with them because he did not know what else to do with him, but Marc told a different story. Tongue firmly in cheek, Marc was to suggest that 'John's Children were visually interesting but it was felt that they needed a kind of Pete Townshend, so obviously they picked on me!' Both versions are feasible, but the true reason, and the initial idea, came from another source. According to the

Simon Napier-Bell and Chris Welch biography, *Marc Bolan: Born to Boogie*, the credit goes to Kit Lambert, co-manager (with Chris Stamp) of the Who. Lambert and Stamp had just formed their own record label, Track Records. The first two acts signed to Track were Jimi Hendrix and John's Children. Lambert, however, had told Napier-Bell that, as part of the package, Marc Bolan should play guitar with the band. Having a record deal on the same label as Jimi Hendrix was exactly the kind of ego trip that suited Bolan, as Hendrix was one of his new heroes.

Supposedly, John's Children were one of the first psychedelic acts of the sixties, although it was their onstage antics that got them noticed more than anything else. They did have minor hits, but their main claim to fame is the title of a faked live album they recorded in 1966. *Orgasm* was banned when advertised in America. The title itself was enough to ensure meltdown in the conservative USA, and the image of the girl on the front cover sealed its fate. The band's vocalist, Andy Ellison, stated that on their first meeting with Marc at Simon Napier-Bell's flat, 'This little guy came walking in with a copy of [Bob Dylan's] *Blonde on Blonde*. We spent the rest of the evening sitting around listening to that and didn't see Marc again until he turned up one evening at the club.'

Chris Townson, drummer with John's Children, also recalled that, before joining the band in March 1966, Marc had never played an electric guitar: 'His first one was a really stodgy old Gibson SG, which Simon [Napier-Bell] bought from Trevor White of the A-Jaes,' he recalled. 'He played it incredibly loudly. His first rehearsal with us was deafening, even by our normal standards! I think the band actually got worse when Marc first joined, because all he did was stand there and make this muddy blurge. It really was a horrible noise.' As to be expected, Marc had a different take on the John's Children period: 'From the beginning I saw my place alongside people like Dylan or Pete Townshend. Only because I've heard Pete, and I've seen Pete, and I've played with Pete, and I know I'm as good as Pete. And he knows I'm as good as he is.'

The band's first release with Bolan was the single 'Desdemona', which he had penned. It was banned by the BBC, reportedly for the mention of the word 'nude' and the line 'Lift up your skirt and fly'. While we can appreciate that Marc was perceived to be in a band of dubious morals – in comparison, say, with the clean-cut image of such bands as Herman's Hermits and the Beatles – these were hardly shocking words and lines. Marc himself said of the single at the time, 'I wrote this one myself, and it took me twenty-five seconds! The story's about . . . a rich girl, and a fellow who lives by the River Seine, all rather complicated and difficult to explain. I would say it's rather slow and moody. The chorus swings. We're hoping it will do very well anyway.'

Later, in an attempt to justify the song's lyric, Marc explained that the line that offended many was nothing more than a narrative of a witch sitting astride her broom before flying off. Reviews were upbeat, *Record Mirror* declaring that the single was 'An intuitive tip for the [Top] Fifty – based on a feeling that this is very commercial though also rather different. Verse is well sung and the chorus, with "answering" voice in the background, is both catchy and full of impact.

Strong guitar in parts and the beat is just right. Rather a refreshing slice of pop.'

Another review, under the banner 'Don't look for trouble', takes a swipe at the hype: 'I know the producers of this disc . . . are worried lest it should be branded a "dirty record". And there is I suppose one phrase which might be misconstrued – but only if you are looking for trouble. I found it a stimulating track – energetic, tingling and vigorous. It has gimmick appeal in the contrast repetition of the title name, and the novelty semi-spoken phrases reminiscent of The Who and The Troggs. And it's lifted all the way through by some berserk drumming.' Owing to the lack of significant airplay, the single, although a minor hit, failed to dent the mainstream charts.

The follow-up, 'Midsummer Night's Scene', marked the end, according to a Mark Paytress feature on John's Children in the September 2002 issue of *MOJO*: 'All of us were in tears because we knew we had a Number One record.'

Marc later explained, 'We were so happy. Next day, we went back to the studio and listened to it, and the guy who was producing had destroyed the song – I walked out and never came back.'

Further bad luck dogged Marc when it appeared that someone 'lost' all his electric equipment, forcing him to turn acoustic. Conflicting accounts later surfaced. Bolan's version was, 'Around the "Desdemona" period I was really getting into guitar playing as a way forward. I abandoned it because they sold my guitar. But, had they not, I would have been an electric guitarist. I would never have been an acoustic guitarist.'

For his part, Simon Napier-Bell says that the equipment got lost in Germany after the band's tour with the Who. Why did Bolan leave the band? Napier-Bell was asked many years later. His reply was in complete contrast to what Marc had stated. 'We were selling records and were getting good audiences, but Marc suddenly decided he didn't want any part of electric music any more.' A recently unearthed post-John's Children recording (and the rumour that Bolan's new band equipment was repossessed) would suggest that what Marc craved was his independence.

What Bolan did want to do, the manager surmised, was 'sit on a rug with a joss stick and an acoustic guitar, indulging his new-found hippiness and long-time fairy-tale fetish, singing numbers that had three chords and sometimes lasted sixteen or seventeen minutes.'

Napier-Bell insisted that Marc's new direction wasn't a gimmick. 'That hippy thing really got to people, and it got to him. I talked it over with him, and told him, "In that case you can't have a manager." The hip-looking managers hadn't yet emerged!' Then, as now, Napier-Bell prefers proper suits and short hair. 'And I couldn't go round saying, "I've got this guy who's a hippy and plays on a rug, and I'm his manager" – already the credibility's gone!'

The recruiting advertisement, placed in *International Times*, epitomised Bolan's self-belief. His band is named in the advert as Tyrannosaurus Rex, the name given to the largest dinosaur ever to walk the Earth. Like the creature itself, though, Marc's new band nearly became extinct – and after the very first gig. Bolan recruited a scratch band of Steve Peregrin Took on drums, Ben Cartland on guitar and an unknown bass player. 'He got a gig at the Electric Garden then put an ad in *Melody Maker* to get the musicians,' remembered Simon Napier-Bell. 'The paper came out on Wednesday, the day of the gig. At three o'clock he was interviewing musicians, at five he was getting ready to go on stage. It was a disaster . . . He just got booed off the stage.'

Steve Peregrin Took, so named after the character from Tolkien's trilogy *The Lord of the Rings*, was the only survivor from that evening's line-up. Those books were a great influence on early Tyrannosaurus Rex material; indeed, the books were part of the staple diet of the hippy movement in the 1960s. The Electric Garden venue itself eventually changed its name to Middle Earth, in a nod to Tolkien's works. The other two musicians chosen from the ad were with Marc only for the length of the disastrous gig. Steve Took elaborated further in a piece by Charles Shaar Murray for *NME*: 'We did one gig at the Electric Garden and the lead guitarist went mad. He started knocking my drum kit about, knocking my cymbals over, I think he thought he was Pete Townshend. After that we decided that we couldn't work with these other two cats.'

Mindful of what had recently occurred, Marc decided that he should move forward with only himself and Steve Took. As a two-piece Tyrannosaurus Rex began to build up a small but welcome head of steam, Marc was again on the lookout for new management. On one occasion, he turned up at Blackhill Enterprises, Pink Floyd's management company. The encounter was not especially fruitful, except that it was there that he met June Child, who was later to become his wife.

'Marc came to see Peter Jenner because he, along with

Andrew King, managed Floyd and he adored Syd Barrett,'
June recalled in an interview with me in the early 1990s.

> Marc felt that, 'If Syd's there, I want to be there too.'
> I looked up and there was this tiny, scruffy little thing,
> in what turned out to be his mother's flying boots, in
> an old school blazer, with the elbows all worn out, a
> very thin silk scarf and greased-back hair, with a sort
> of frizzy bit at the front. 'I've come to see Peter Jenner'
> were his first words to me. I buzzed through and told
> Peter that somebody called Marc Bolan was here to see
> him, and in Marc toddled. I was sitting there typing
> when I had this incredible feeling in my head, almost
> like static electricity; then it was gone and I continued
> typing. Marc re-emerged some time later and I made
> him a cup of tea, and we talked and talked and talked.
> Suddenly he said, 'Oh, I must go,' and off he went,
> back to Wimbledon.

June carried on with her work for all of two hours. Then, the
phone rang. 'Marc was on the line, asking urgently, "Could
you come over? I have to speak to you."' June assumed
that this request had something to do with the meeting
he had had earlier with Peter Jenner, and with Peter's OK
she took the Bentley owned by Pink Floyd to drive over to
Wimbledon:

> I remember it was a beautiful summer day. When
> Marc opened the door, that same static electric buzz
> came into my head. Marc just looked at me and said,

'Would you like some muesli?' and I remember my stunned breathless response of, 'Oh, yes, please.' We sat out on this piece of grass, eating muesli and talking. Then Marc said, 'I've got something for you,' and he reached inside his pocket and pulled out this folded piece of paper. When I opened it, there was the most beautiful love poem. I looked at him and he said, 'I'm in love with you,' and I said, 'Oh, well, all right.' I was quite speechless but I knew it was right.

Marc and June spent that evening and the next four nights sleeping in June's van on Wimbledon Common, until they found a bedsit in Notting Hill's Blenheim Crescent. Theirs was to prove an uncommonly close and fruitful relationship that lasted for years.

At this time, Marc was developing another relationship that was to have far-reaching consequences. John Peel has helped pave the way to success for many acts over a long and illustrious career: Adam and the Ants, the Smiths, Blur, the Clash and the Undertones to name just a few. So it comes as no great surprise to find Peel entwined with the early fortunes of Tyrannosaurus Rex. Peel had already heard Marc through 'Desdemona', penned by the John's Children Bolan. On his show, *The Perfumed Garden*, just days before all the pirate radio stations were banned from airing in the UK, a colleague from Radio London, Peter Farrak, had loaned him 'The Wizard' and 'The Third Degree' from his own collection.

As Rob Chapman explains in his 2002 feature for *MOJO*:

It's clear from Peel's on-air comments that he was unaware of when these records had been first released, and strangely enough Peel did not make the connection between Bolan and John's Children. Bolan heard the broadcast and mailed Peel an acetate of two early Tyrannosaurus Rex demos, 'Highways' and 'Misty Mist'. After playing 'Highways' at 3:55 a.m. on the final *Perfumed Garden* all-nighter on 14 August 1967, Peel excitedly declared, 'What a voice that is. That's Marc Bolan who I'm going to go and see as soon as the opportunity presents itself. I've got to meet him and find out where that strange voice comes from.'

Peel had been impressed enough to give them airplay; after all, it was possible to get away with playing material from innovative new bands on pirate radio that commercial stations would ignore: that was half the fun. In *Marc Bolan: A Tribute*, a quote from Peel shows his genuine affection for Marc: 'I liked him as a human being and I liked his music. From that time on, whenever I had a gig anywhere, I would ask Marc and Steve to go along and play.' And the reactions to the acoustic duo? 'Often the people who were running the gig were not terribly pleased about it, because they didn't like people sitting on the stage banging children's instruments and singing in a bizarre manner,' Peel admitted.

Tyrannosaurus Rex gigged at Middle Earth in Convent Garden as support to John Peel and were invited back again and again. 'I was billed over them,' says Peel, 'then it all started to change. They were Tyrannosaurus Rex introduced by John Peel, which, of course, is the way it should have been.'

Marc was beginning to see signs of improvement with his music and to find a genuine following at last. Tyrannosaurus Rex played colleges as well as all the open-air festivals that were then becoming so popular and the duo were to appear at the first free Hyde Park festival in 1968. These years saw the full bloom of flower power and the hippy movement, with which Steve Took was more heavily involved than Marc. Took was later to say that Marc was, for a while at least, a good hippy. They would sit around for hours discussing how the world needed changing and, while Took felt he wanted to get more into this, Marc had other ideas that evolved as the band became more popular. The underground movement was no longer a priority for him.

Very much a unit, but still without management, Bolan and Took continued gigging. One evening, during the autumn of 1967, they were playing at the UFO Club in London's Tottenham Court Road. As it turned out, it was at this event that Tony Visconti was introduced to Marc's music. It was to prove the most important introduction for the career and aspirations of the young singer – and also boosted the production career of the fast-rising Visconti.

Tony Visconti was born in Brooklyn, New York, in 1944. His early aspiration was to be a musician – not in rock 'n' roll (he lost interest in it after the demise of such pioneering greats as Buddy Holly) but in jazz. Visconti married young and with his wife formed a duo called Tony and Siegrid; they had a recording contract with RCA, for whom they cut two singles. Visconti wrote his own material and recorded a great deal at home. His boss, Howard Richmond of the Richmond Organisation, agreed to let him spend two months in London to study record producing. The Richmond family owned a sister company in England called Essex Music and Denny Cordell, who worked for Essex, had already asked Visconti to come over and work as his assistant. Cordell had been searching for an American producer to consolidate his love for the kind of sounds then being created in US studios.

By the time Visconti got his first look at Marc at UFO, the producer had worked in Denny Cordell's Essex studio on hit albums and singles for Procol Harum and the Move. That evening at the club, he found himself among a couple of hundred people, silent and mesmerised, listening to a strange little pixie type who sat cross-legged on stage with a beatnik partner playing children's musical pipes and banging bongos. Intrigued, and keen to talk business, Tony approached Steve Took after the gig and began to introduce himself. 'Man, I'm too bummed out to talk to you. See him, he's the one who does the business,' Took interrupted. Visconti had approached Steve first because he found Marc too intimidating. 'I didn't see a musician,' recalled Visconti much later, talking to journalist Mick Brown. 'I saw a star.' His initial judgement was confirmed when he did as Steve suggested. Marc was almost dismissive when Tony introduced himself. After all, the singer enthused, Tony was the seventh producer who had approached him in the past few weeks – and didn't he know that even John Lennon wanted to work with him? 'Leave me your number, anyway' was Bolan's curt reply.

Marc phoned Visconti the following day at Essex Music and asked if he could come and play to him. Within the hour, he arrived with Steve and they performed the entire set from the previous night's gig on the floor of Denny Cordell's office. Cordell was confounded, but sufficiently impressed to agree to the signing of Tyrannosaurus Rex 'as our "token" underground group', as Visconti noted in his 2007 autobiography.

Regal Zonophone, a record label owned by Essex Music and distributed by EMI, released Tyrannosaurus Rex's first album, *My People Were Fair and Had Sky in Their Hair . . . But Now They're Content to Wear Stars on Their Brows*, and the single 'Debora', recorded for around £250 combined. 'This is ever so clever, ever so different – and I hope ever so that it makes the charts,' exclaimed one reviewer. 'When something really off-beat and unusual comes along, one raises a cheer.' Released on 19 April 1968, the debut single took many people by surprise with the driving rhythm of the acoustic guitar and Marc's much stronger vocals. It did reasonably well in the UK charts, registering at No. 34 in the recognised Top Forty published weekly by the BBC. The flipside, 'Child Star', was a track taken from *My People Were Fair . . .*, released on 7 July that year. 'This complex, catchy, ad-lib-type single gets three cheers from me,' raved one critic. Another review was in a similar vein: 'A versatile and very under rated group, which discerning listeners will have heard many times on *Top Gear*. This is a fascinating disc debut that's probably much too offbeat to succeed. [It] battles along at a hectic pace, with acoustic guitar and bongo. All very clever and intricate – probably too complex to register.'

Reflecting later on that first album, Marc was asked whether he liked the production. 'No, it was bad,' he replied.

Perhaps the reality was that Tony Visconti simply was not 'into' what the music was all about. 'No. Tony was really with us, and it was the first LP he'd ever produced and it was done at Advision on a nine-track – the first in the country – and they didn't know how to use it. The stereo was awful. When we were doing it, it sounded good, but, when it was on record, it sounded very thin and nasty. But we did it in two or three sessions – the whole thing only cost £200 to make, and "Debora" only cost £30. I like the feeling of the first LP but as a production, I can't listen to it.'

One unaccredited journalist from *ZigZag* magazine questioned Marc: 'Tyrannosaurus Rex were folky more than anything else in the early days and the first album had a charm and simplicity of its own. I'm intrigued by a lot of songs on that album, but "Child Star" and "Graceful Fat Sheba" particularly. Were these based on reality?'

'No,' responded Marc, 'I just liked the idea of a young classical star writing incredible melodies at five. But they killed him, and when he was dead, they didn't see what his music was about anyway. It was going to be a book . . . but I've never read an article about anything and thought "Wow, I must use that." Not consciously anyway.'

It is clear to me that the influence of Tolkien was very strongly represented in Marc's work up until 1971 and the release of *Electric Warrior*. The elves, dwarfs and dragons were a foundation, an ever-present twisting and turning kaleidoscope of dreamlike sequences within the lyrics. In his book *The Wizard's Gown – Rewoven*, however, Tony Stringfellow dismisses the Tolkien influence in favour of the writings of C S Lewis and *The Chronicles of Narnia*.

Stringfellow states, 'Marc did not take to Tolkien's Hobbit tale, despite his earlier works being described by many as Tolkienesque . . . [T]here are little if no Tolkien references in Bolan's work but he did embrace Lewis's Narnia.' This seems strange to me, in light of the fact that Stringfellow himself then quotes one of Bolan's earlier poems, which clearly nods to Tolkien's books: 'Tipped for stardom, by goblin unknown / knowin' maybe, I'd seen some ring (but don't worry 'cos Gandalf sees all).'

Visconti had his own feelings about the first album he produced for the band and adds further confirmation of the role Tolkien played. Bolan told the producer, 'If you're gonna record me, you gotta read these,' and presented him with the *Lord of the Rings* trilogy and *The Hobbit*. In Mick Brown's article for the *Telegraph*, from 2002, Visconti notes that, although *The Lord of the Rings* fascinated Bolan, he had not actually read the books, as he was dyslexic. 'Lying in bed together,' the producer recalled, 'June read the three volumes out loud to Bolan – and *The Hobbit* too.' Visconti added that he felt, 'She filled in all the pieces that were missing in his life. June became his lover, chauffeur, minder, mentor, and eventually, his wife.'

In *The Record Producers*, by John Tobler and Stuart Grundy, Visconti had this to say about the album and his pick of the tracks on it:

I've still got lots of favourites, but the song I like most is an adorable little track, called 'Strange Orchestras'. We only had four days to make that album, and whereas the other tracks were done quite quickly and frantically, and with the minimum of overdubs, 'Strange Orchestras' was our only attempt at doing something slick, where you have these little surprising sounds appearing now and then. It always conjures up for me an image of a tiny elfin orchestra, little people playing tiny little instruments. There are more beautiful songs on the album, like 'Afghan Woman' and the title track, but I still get a thrill listening to 'Strange Orchestras' on headphones.

The album appealed to a growing army of fans – mainly hippies and arty types. One music paper on 20 July suggested, 'Most of the tracks are a kind of jug-band psychedelia with a set of vocals which sound like the earliest blues recordings. Phrasing is deliberately vague but the lyrics are worth listening to. The overall sound is samey, but then, if you like one track, there are enough variations for you to like the lot. Original, deserves to be a big seller, maybe it will be.' Another review screamed the headline, 'Tyrannosaurus Rex – way ahead yet out of date!' Oozing reverence, it proclaimed, 'Marc is one of the most prolific composers we know and the strength of this album lies in his excellent, totally individual songs of love, beauty, fantasy and nature. And then Marc says that for him, this album is months out of date! Which bodes extremely well for the future.'

My People Were Fair . . . reached a respectable No. 15 in the UK charts, yet Tyrannosaurus Rex failed to have any Top Twenty hit singles over the next two and a half years. I would suggest that the reason for this is that each record format had its market, fuelled by quite a stuffy attitude towards singles releases. I remember as a youngster hanging out with hippy friends who would not be caught dead buying singles. These purchasing trends were also coloured by simple economics, with albums being much better value than singles and easily within reach of the average fan. When T. Rex's hits began, several years later, the situation was reversed: youngsters bought singles but could not afford the albums so easily.

Their newfound success made a big difference to life in general. One minute, June and Marc had put Marc's guitar in hock to find the rent of £3 8s 6d (£3.42) a week; the next, Tyrannosaurus Rex were getting £20 a gig. More success was to follow. On 6 July, the band appeared at the Woburn Music Festival in Bedfordshire among the contemporary rock-music elite of Family, Donovan and the Jimi Hendrix Experience. At the free festival in Hyde Park on 29 June, Tyrannosaurus Rex played to more than eight thousand fans alongside acts such as Pink Floyd, Roy Harper and Jethro Tull. Within two months of these gigs and the release of the first album, the band could negotiate fees of over £100 a night.

On 23 August 1968, the follow-up single 'One Inch Rock' hit the shops; the flipside was 'Salamanda Palaganda' from an album newly completed but not yet released. The single broke into the UK Top Thirty, albeit peaking at only No. 28, but it gave Marc his first taste of minor chart success. People were beginning to take notice of Tyrannosaurus Rex; slowly, the Bolan juggernaut was gathering speed. Writing in *Disc and Music Echo*, Penny Valentine said of the new single, 'It has taken me much longer than all those hip people who have been digging them for ages to appreciate this group. I now admit I find their sound rather endearing, certainly very individual, and totally, totally fascinating.'

On her first impressions of Marc, she stated, 'He's much smaller and delicate looking close to than I had suspected,' while admitting, 'I'm glad they put a title on this because I couldn't understand a thing he was singing about.' Another unaccredited journalist wrote 'It's happy, light hearted and thoroughly infectious. [. . .] All credit to the band for coming up with something that's undemanding, good fun and blues chasing.'

The second album with a title equally as challenging as the first, *Prophets, Seers & Sages: The Angel of the Ages*, was released on 14 October, and was met mainly with good reviews. The enchanting voice of Bolan once more mystified many, yet left the listener wanting to know and hear more. As one review put it:

It appears that you either cannot hear enough of the band, or else you hate them with a deep and deadly loathing. For the former the new album will be a joy and a delight, the latter will find it boring, or offensive or pretentious or whatever as all the rest of their work. Be that as it may, a lot more people are being turned on to Steve Peregrin Took and Marc Bolan's songs of beauty and happiness in their own style. Marc can afford to be better pleased with this second album than their first because it is in fact quite excellent. Should, and undoubtedly will, sell many thousands – and quite deservedly so too!

Quite incredibly, however, it did not chart. For reasons still not understood, the album did not live up to Bolan's expectations from the gathering momentum of popular support, which continued regardless.

The year 1969 opened with the release of 'Pewter Suitor' on 14 January. This, their third single, failed to register at all on the charts. Bolan was perplexed but not demoralised, as the failure of the single did not cross over to the gigs. This topsy-turvy journey was best summed up by a reviewer at the time: 'I've never really doubted their talent – only mine in not knowing where on earth they are going. But their name liveth, despite various ups and downs . . . rather a good song idea.'

Tyrannosaurus Rex were increasingly in demand. Marc, now more eager than ever to reach a growing legion of converts, appeared at London's Queen Elizabeth Hall on 13 January. Chris Welch reported on the gig in complimentary terms overall: 'A handful of musical fairy dust was thrown in to the air at London's Queen Elizabeth Hall on Monday, which baffled some and choked others. Tyrannosaurus Rex with John Peel at the wand, conducted us on a tour of a land of rattles, plinks, plonks and poetry, and the applause was rapturous. Some young mods in the audience were not quite sure how to take John [Peel] reading poetry to prove the existence of the fairies, but remained politely silent.'

Tyrannosaurus Rex performed four gigs in February, appearing first at the Birmingham Town Hall on 15 February, followed by Fairfield Hall in Croydon (16th) Manchester Free Trade Hall (22nd) and Bristol's Colston Hall (23rd). March continued in the same vein, with Marc and Steve appearing at the Philharmonic Hall in Liverpool on the first of the month and ending the tour at the Dome in Brighton seven days later.

Just prior to the release of the third album, *Unicorn*, in May 1969, an article by Derek Boltwood appeared in *Record Mirror* under the heading 'From the Underworld'. It was a piece about underground groups, but Boltwood displayed prescience, both in recognising the potential superstar who played before him and in being, I would venture to suggest, the first journalist to abbreviate the name Tyrannosaurus Rex to 'T. Rex'. 'The audience is not exactly hostile or aggressive but it certainly doesn't know quite what to expect,' he noted. When the duo appear on stage, the feedback from the crowd is neither good nor bad, indifferent in parts – summed up by Boltwood as, 'We've heard of you and heard your albums, now let's see what you're really like.'

Of course, the initiated have seen Tyrannosaurus Rex before, so they know what's coming and they applaud in happy anticipation. Boltwood sums up the gig in a final paragraph: 'Strangely, although an automatic labelling machine would say: introvert music, T. Rex music is extrovert and becoming more so. Easier to be involved than stay cool . . . thus the reason for success now, I feel.'

When *Unicorn* was released on 18 May, it was regarded by some of the press as Tyrannosaurus Rex's finest album to date. The band's songs were often criticised as sounding too similar, but it was also generally acknowledged that 'even though the sounds were the same, what [Tyrannosaurus Rex] did was totally distinctive and a pleasant antidote to the constant deluge of loud electric music'.

Unicorn, it was said, 'broadened their scope. Bring in harmonisation, lip organ, piano and bass without losing their characteristic child-like simplicity.'

'Why did you have that piano on "Cat Black"?' *ZigZag* asked Marc. 'That song was really inspired by those "Runaround Sue" sort of songs – the chords and so on,' he replied, 'and I wanted to do that sort of melody with nice words. I brought the piano in so that people who are into rock 'n' roll piano could relate to it a bit.'

Marc had much more time to put his ideas together – the royalties from previous releases ensured that. He also seemed to have changed direction quite subtly, however, with the Tolkien influences still there, plain to hear, but with a distinct difference in the way the songs were delivered. Some of the naïveté of the first two albums had disappeared and in its place was a maturity and confidence in the way the material was produced. 'Overall,' one uncredited review stated, '*Unicorn* is a more acceptable LP for mass appeal than previous ones.' The album reached No. 12 in the UK charts.

In conversation with the journalist Michael March, Bolan revealed that he had always considered *Unicorn* 'a very spiritual album'. There was nothing about any of the religions that inspired Marc and there was none of them that he felt he could align himself to. His music was steeped in paganism and 'the ability to understand that it's the Earth that's important and that from the Earth comes your food and from the skies comes your inspiration'.

Later, in 1969, he was to reveal an even greater insight into his spiritual side. Marc and Steve Peregrin Took spent time in Cornwall and Wales, and it was during this time of tranquillity and peace that Marc felt himself at one with nature. He confided to friends that *Unicorn* was an expression from deep within his soul. It was at this point that Bolan started taking also a much greater interest in studio production. No longer happy simply to lay down tracks, he now wanted to produce bigger sounds, more intelligent little embellishments, and tracks such as 'Romany Soup' became epic walls of sound.

In an interview with *ZigZag* magazine, he boasted that 'Romany Soup' 'has twenty-two tracks [layers] on it and took five hours to mix. And, on the "Unicorn" track, the drums gave me a real buzz, because I wanted to get a Phil Spector sound. I don't know how well it came off. The songs on *Prophets . . .* are very much like the songs on *Unicorn*, but younger.' In a much later interview, he would tell Michael March, 'I was at a very uncommercial stage and "Cat Black" is a pop song. Most of the things on *Prophets . . .* weren't at all. They were woodland songs. I wrote most of them in the country. They're sad country sorts. Whereas *Unicorn* is a combination of the two. It's like *Prophets . . .* but I've used instruments. I've tried to make it more interesting because I need more sounds. The things I'm doing now are very electric.'

'What is Romany soup?' Marc is asked.

'It's something we bought in Cornwall. It's made by Knorr or someone, and it really tasted a groove.'

Marc the songwriter became Bolan the poet when Lupus Music, an independent publisher owned by his then manager, Brian Morrison, published a book of poetry titled *The Warlock of Love*. It was not really to sell in great numbers until T. Rex became more popular a couple of years later. Initially, the book was available only by mail order with a retail price of 14s 6d (72.5p), which included postage and packing.

With *Unicorn* acknowledged as the band's best album thus far, Marc turned his attention to the follow-up single. He was beginning to feel that the acoustic developments he had made with his music, and for which Tyrannosaurus Rex were famous, were in need of some tweaking. Fortunately, improved finances were to allow him to experiment more and this included the acquisition of an electric guitar and the consequent development of a new sound for the band, unleashed on an unsuspecting United Kingdom on 25 July. Steve Took remarked to *NME* in October 1972, 'I got into playing guitar again, playing bass, and we did an electric single "King of the Rumbling Spires".' It was described by one reviewer as being more than just a song: 'This was a poem set to music. The lyrics deep, thought provoking and enigmatic.' Another proclaimed that, 'This is Bolan Child's most commercial production to date and, with Took rocking feverishly on regular drums, they could easily crack the chart problem.'

Not everyone agreed, though: '"Debora" was great. But on this they've got too much backing – it's overloaded. It's messy and the only words you can hear is the title.' Aggression had replaced the softer tones of the band's earlier offerings. 'King of the Rumbling Spires' stunned many of Bolan's growing legion of fans, who appeared not to like what they heard: the single reached only No. 44 in the UK charts – and for just one week before slipping away again.

Come the end of summer 1969, Bolan announced that Tyrannosaurus Rex were to tour America. However, cracks were starting to appear in the musical relationship and direction between Marc and Took. During the recording of *Unicorn* it was obvious to Marc that there would be a parting of the ways. 'I just grew apart from Steve Took,' Marc later reflected.

The duo tried to rehearse for two whole days before going to America, but nothing materialised of any useful significance. Tyrannosaurus Rex went to America in the worst possible frame of mind, having decided to split. Bolan admitted. 'I got to New York and got beaten up in the Village on three successive occasions and retired to my hotel room. In Seattle, I got shot at by some insane sniper and the whole trip became a nightmare. In short, the tour was a disaster and signalled the end for the Bolan–Took partnership. I've been asked Steve Took's reason for leaving – it was just that we didn't communicate at all.'

There was never any chemistry in the true sense of the word between Marc and Steve. Marc would write the songs, then play them to Steve, and they would just agree on the finished formula. Marc wrote the songs on *A Beard of Stars* while on tour in the States. All that time, Marc was rehearsing on his own, laying down the demos onto a cassette player, forging a trail by himself.

On returning to England – minus Steve Took, who remained in the USA – Marc announced to the press that the split was a mutual thing and there had been 'no bad scenes'. Initially, the announcement had a negative impact: booking agents stopped asking for Tyrannosaurus Rex, thinking it was all over for the band. Marc rallied as ever, but the almost throwaway, laidback approach to the breakup with Took hid the true extent of the problems. June later revealed, in *Marc Bolan: A*

Tribute, by Ted Dicks and Paul Platz, about resultant parting of the ways:

> Steve Took was very heavily into acid, but very heavily – not just an indulger: he'd be taking two or three trips a day. He became just like a vegetable and on stage – a stage about as big as you'd get in a tiny club that seated about one hundred people – he would suddenly start taking off his clothes and beating himself with belts and things like that. When you've only got two people on stage, a guitar player and a bongo player, you can't have the bongo player not playing bongos as you're left with only an acoustic guitar. There was no electric guitar then. We left Steve in America; we abandoned him. He met this chick and said he didn't think he was coming back, so we just said for him to go. We came back to England, not knowing what we were going to do.

While June and Marc returned to England shattered by the prospect that Tyrannosaurus Rex was, for the moment at least, a nonentity, with hindsight it heralded a new era for the singer. An advert that he placed in *Melody Maker* for a 'nice gentle guy to play bongos' became redundant when a new character arrived on the scene – one who, it was suggested, might be more important visually than as a musical partner.

Mickey Finn was born in Thornton Heath, Surrey, in 1947. At nearby Rockmount Secondary School, the focus of his interests became music, art and motorbikes. His rock-music influences were the familiar key artists of the 1950s:

Elvis Presley, Buddy Holly and Little Richard. It was in his passion for art, however, that Mickey thought his future lay. He attended the Croydon College of Art in the mid-1960s, registering for a four-year course. There, his work was considered good, but not his attitude. After just eleven months he quit and moved to London, where he became involved in psychedelia and the flower-power movement. It was the time of the Beatles' *Sgt. Pepper* album, and Mickey's circle of friends included fashion models, painters and photographers. He was in a band called Hapshash and the Coloured Coat, which folded soon after he joined. He then pursued a variety of artistic interests, but it was while Mickey was painting internal murals that a shared friend mentioned his name to Marc.

Mickey Finn was dark and extremely good-looking, a perfect match for the elfin Bolan. He was introduced to him as a painter, as a fellow artiste, which Marc found most appealing. It was only much later that Mickey admitted he had been working as a house painter and decorator. An asset such as musicianship might have been considered vital, but that did not seem to matter to Marc at the time. Mickey could not sing and certainly had limited musical abilities, but he quite simply looked the business.

Marc and Mickey went into retreat in Wales, where Finn had to learn a great deal in a short space of time. Astonishingly, and as a reflection of their joint determination, on 17 November the new Tyrannosaurus Rex duo recorded John Peel's BBC radio show *Top Gear*, for transmission four days later. It was the first public appearance of Marc's new partner and, equally relevant, the first time the band's heavier, electric-guitar-oriented songs were heard. On the day this session was transmitted, Marc also introduced Mickey to his first live audience at the Manchester Free Trade Hall, at the start of a five-date introduction tour.

T·REX

**RIDE A WHITE SWAN/IS IT LOVE/
SUMMERTIME BLUES**

BUG I
TRIPLE "A" SIDE STEREO SINGLE

THE MOVE

**WHEN ALICE COMES BACK TO THE
FARM/WHAT?**

BUG 2
STEREO SINGLE

Distributed by E·M·I

70 Old Compton Street London WI
01-734 0853   01-437 9506

DAVID PLATZ   KIT LAMBERT   CHRIS STAMP

1970

MARC BOLAN

In 1970, Tyrannosaurus Rex were reborn and with their renaissance came a new single. For me personally, 'By the Light of a Magical Moon' was a mixture of electric rock and a spellbinding lyric of enchanted moments. As a fan, I feel it should have been Bolan's first major hit, but the opposite proved to be the case: the press did not seem to care for the single, and it prompted the first critical rumblings – that the band, thus far so well received as a live entity and appreciated for the albums, were selling out, their sound swamped by too much electric guitar.

'Rex is looked upon by many as an album group. Maybe so,' surmised one uncredited reviewer 'though I am confident [the band's] turn in the singles chart will come. But whether it will be with this disc is a moot point. It's hauntingly insistent, has colourful lyrics . . . a throbbing beat and highlights some sizzling guitar work.'

Some journalists, however, pleaded for the single to be supported: 'This is a gentle, moody piece of light hearted writing, with good vocal line and some intriguing guitar spasms. At least try it, please!' Fans, who had proved so faithful to the band at gigs and in album sales, took little or no heed. They turned their back on the single. Bolan, it was suggested, should return to his roots. In an act of petulance, Marc declared that he was 'giving up' on singles in the UK and henceforth would make only albums. He became particularly agitated, feeling that the press had never been off his back. With few exceptions, Marc felt he had rarely been taken seriously enough. And, as far as he was concerned, his music was not made for them, but for the fans. 'I don't read the reviews, anyway,' Marc was later to quip.

A Beard of Stars surfaced on the Regal Zonophone label on 22 March 1970. It was to be the last album released under the name Tyrannosaurus Rex. The content of the album proved to be too much for press and fans alike, although it can be argued that it left nobody in any doubt as to where Marc was heading musically. The album contained a mixture of whimsical, gentle tracks with more than a hint of romance: 'Prelude', 'Organ Blues' and 'Lofty Skies' were all enchanting. The real shock came, however, with 'Fist Heart Mighty Dawn Dart', 'Dragon's Ear' and the quite stunning 'Elemental Child', a track that would make many fans catch their breath. It was the track that for me, as a fan, defined the arrival of Marc Bolan the rock-'n'-roll artist and it was a move not uncommon among artists who trucked alongside him in that era. The singer himself thought *A Beard of Stars* the best album he'd ever done, conceding: 'I suppose there is more electric guitar . . . I've been staying down at Eric Clapton's home quite a bit recently and you can't be around Eric and not be influenced.'

Adverts for the LP showed Marc with his white Fender Stratocaster, while *Melody Maker* declared, 'Bolan goes electric: Never has the band sounded so heavy or exciting . . . "Elemental Child" will come as a considerable surprise. It features Marc's untutored but energetic and groovy heavy rock guitar work.' Tyrannosaurus Rex introduced the new material at various gigs, including Pop Proms at the Roundhouse, in London's Camden Town, in April. Finn would ride his 650cc motorbike over to Bolan's Ladbroke Grove flat to rehearse. Marc mused, 'I think we'll have a bass player at some point, but not just yet . . . there'll come a point where if I want to do a long guitar solo, or just allow something to happen like that, then we'll need a bass player for that number.' The perceived evolution from hippy to rock 'n' roll most certainly lies within the music that Marc generated through *A Beard of Stars*. It was clear that Marc was always going to evolve and, thankfully for him, time was very much on his side.

Later, Marc himself conceded that. 'I was always going to do it, you know? Even when we did "Debora", it was always, "Next week I'll plug my Stratocaster in." But I couldn't play well enough then to make the noises that I wanted to hear. Our new things are rock and roll . . . all twelve bars.'

With the introduction of a heavier, pounding rhythm, driven along with power chords and frenetic solos, there was one element that remained constant in the songs. As Rikki

Rooksby observed in *Guitarist* magazine years later, they were 'still clearly rooted in the Tolkienesque landscape of Marc's imagination. This fusion of rock and roll with Middle Earth is probably Marc's most distinctive gift to English rock music.' Rooksby also singled out the guitar work for praise: 'Some of Bolan's best lead is heard on the album, the wah-wah solo in "Lofty Skies" and "Elemental Child", with its reality-is-on-the-blink whammy-bar pauses and an extended coda with heavy damping of the strings.'

Singles can sometimes confuse the record-buying public, and that was certainly the case back in the early 1970s, when the albums produced by many bands were far heavier, more complex and more demanding than their 45s. Tyrannosaurus Rex would feature their latest single as the last track at live gigs to warm the audience up to the new groove. These new songs highlighted just how far he had progressed in his ability as a serious guitarist, yet he continued to be haunted by press resistance to his capabilities. In an era that had spawned the likes of Eric Clapton and Jimi Hendrix, Bolan sometimes found it difficult to be taken seriously by the music press. Ironically, the more successful he became, the harder he found it. 'He was there to be shot at more and more,' an exasperated June Feld summed up. Not all the reviews were bad, of course. Picking up on the new electric-guitar influence on *A Beard of Stars*, as *Melody Maker* noted, 'A rock and roll influence on Tyrannosaurus Rex is much in evidence on "Woodland Bop"[,] a bright little ditty which should have gnomes in the country[side] jiving in their glades.'

A Beard of Stars did reasonably well, finally resting at a credible No. 21 in the UK album charts. Bolan now felt he was in the ascendancy, and confidently dedicated the next five months to writing and recording tracks for yet another new album. In an interview with me in 1991, reflecting on that period, June said with a smile, 'Marc changed, not only in his musical direction but also in his own persona. Never one to lack in confidence, he matured in stature and he understood finally the concept of who he was and who he would be.'

One summer evening, Marc recorded a demo of a song that was originally meant to be included on the new album. June Feld: 'We were living in Marble Arch then, in one of those high-rise "security prisons". And it had a spare bedroom, which we'd "egg-boxed" [to reduce the noise of Marc playing his guitars or listening back to reel-to-reel tapes of rough studio mixes] . . . He used to get this weird look in his eyes . . . this sort of third-dimensional . . . spaced look. And he suddenly jumped up and he whisked off. He said, "I've got to go" . . . [from the room next door she heard] all this plinking and plonking. And I had the television on and I was reading . . . and he said, "Come and listen to this!" . . . And there it was: "Ride a White Swan". And then the first thing he always asked – I don't know if he ever asked anybody else this – "Does it sound like anything else? Does it sound like anything you've ever heard before?"' June offered opinions and suggestions; Marc made some changes and called her back to hear the revised track.

'It's great, wonderful!' June enthused. 'I'm sure it'll be a hit.'

'Doesn't sound like anybody else?'

'No, it doesn't sound like anybody else.'

The following morning he played it back and decided to go to the studio that same day so that Tony Visconti could hear it.

At this juncture, there was also another change, albeit one that had evolved via the press in recent times as journalists struggled with the lengthy name 'Tyrannosaurus Rex'. As part of the sessions for the band's soon-to-be-released fourth album, Visconti had to write out the titles of tracks and artist names on the master-tape boxes. After a while, he tired of laboriously writing out the band's name in full and, at the end of a session one day, he abbreviated the name to T. Rex. On seeing this, Marc initially insisted that the name be written out in full. For the moment, Visconti let it drop and left it for some time until one day he repeated the words 'T. Rex' and Marc made no comment. When advance copies arrived of the single 'Ride a White Swan', the label simply stated T. Rex.

Reviewing the single for *Rolling Stone*, Paul Gambaccini predicted, '"Ride a White Swan" is a good record, a clever record, and a soon-to-be-successful record . . . Marc Bolan and Mickey Finn have released one of the most likeable 45s . . . The initial impression that the record must be turning at the wrong speed is discounted by trying different speeds, making it sound more bizarre. The high notes, nonsense syllables and guttural noises are all Bolan and Finn's.'

Gambaccini also made a telling point about the band's newly developed pop sensibilities: 'Never let it be said the fellows aren't conscious of the time limitations of radio stations with tight playlists.' Explaining further, he points out, 'Not only have they kept "Ride a White Swan" down to 2:15, they've shortened their name to T. Rex.'

'Ride a White Swan' was Marc's first Top Twenty hit single. It was also the first single to be issued with two tracks on the flipside, including the band's only non-Bolan composition to date, Eddie Cochran's *'Summertime Blues'*. The single's release coincided with the relaunch of Regal Zonophone as Fly.

The first tour as T. Rex began at Nottingham's Albert Hall on 9 October 1970, barely a week after the single came out. In what should be considered as one of the shrewdest business moves ever made, tickets to the gigs were set at the pre-decimal price of just 10s (50p), which assured that the band would attract a young audience. Reflecting on that day, journalist B P Fallon remarked: '[Rexmania] broke. That's when the rock-'n'-roll tide turned and Boley started becoming a rock-'n'-roll icon. We talked about it after the gig. It was an inexplicable feeling.' To the considerable bemusement of the older, more 'serious' fans, young girls started to appear at the gigs. The screaming gathered pace; many of the established old-school disciples found the change too much to handle. To them, Marc had truly sold out: he was now becoming a pop star and while many of them resigned themselves to the fact – they could hardly begrudge him a single hit after so many years – they still found the new look and sound unpalatable.

Initially, however, 'Ride a White Swan' did not pick up airplay. Was it down to the DJs' reluctance to play the song, or bloody-mindedness on the parts of the people who decided what did and did not get played on the dreaded BBC playlist? Radio plugger Anya Wilson recalled, 'I first met Marc and Mickey when "Ride a White Swan" was on release – it hadn't been getting many plays on Radio 1 and I was asked [by B P Fallon] if I'd work on it. We were trying for all the plays

we could get and I fixed up an interview on Radio 1 Club –
alongside a Radio 1 Club interview with Marc, during which
"Ride a White Swan" got a single play.' Reportedly, on the
strength of that interview, 20,000 copies were sold in record
stores the following day. Wilson had done her job well. The
single now appeared on the playlists.

Success brought fresh problems for Marc, specifically
concerning the sound at gigs. In the studios, this was not
a problem as he could simply overdub as necessary, while
Visconti played bass guitar and the string sections added
their meat to the bone to create the big sound. On tour,
it was another matter. Although Marc had tried to avoid
having to expand the band's line-up, there was no getting
away from the fact that kids arrived at gigs expecting to
hear what they had just left at home on their record players.
Visconti – who had played bass on the recording of 'Ride
a White Swan' and on stage for two gigs – finally swayed
Marc to add more band members.

First to arrive was bass guitarist Steve Currie, who joined
T. Rex midway through the British autumn tour. Currie was
born in Grimsby in 1947. Bass was to become the love of his
life and he went on to play around Grimsby in the evenings
with a band called Rumble, appearing every weekend at a jazz
club in the city. Currie's family had hoped that he would take
up medicine, but he couldn't pass his English exams and so
failed to get into medical school. He did become a member of
the Chartered Institute of Ship Brokers, but decided instead to
pursue a career in rock.

Currie moved down to London in the late 1960s with the
rest of his band to seek fame and fortune, but they all found

life extremely hard in the capital and increasing debts left them with little choice but to return to Grimsby. Currie, however, had come south with his girlfriend, who had a steady daytime job and was willing to provide him with financial support. For a while, therefore, he decided to stay in London to give things a chance to improve.

It was to be a life-changing decision. Flipping casually through the pages of a music paper, he saw an advertisement for a bass guitarist. On answering the ad, he found himself in the company of Marc Bolan. His first reaction to meeting Bolan was one of dismay, as Currie was, by his own admission, a rocker. 'Jesus Christ' he thought initially, 'a jingle-jangle type!' Yet, in an interview, Currie revealed, 'I was doing auditions all the time. Much of the bands didn't have much to offer and I wasn't prepared to take on another dead horse and kick it alive. When I found out I was auditioning for T. Rex, I had strange visions of a guy with an acoustic guitar making wailing sounds. We began playing "Jewel" and it was like we'd been playing together for twenty years. It was amazing, funky music and just what I wanted to play.'

As the T. Rex phenomenon gathered pace, so did the size of the equipment needed to satisfy the visual and musical roadshow. Marc was proud to have the only stereo sound capability when on tour. The bigger the venues, the more financial clout Marc was able to exert and the more T. Rex were able to deliver what the fans wanted most: a night to remember. He said of the live sound, 'When you see their faces when they hear our stereo sound, it's really a turn-on. It helps the atmosphere at gigs and can be used to good effect on guitar things. Gets the sound zooming around.'

On 11 December 1970, during the week that 'Ride a White Swan' hit the No. 6 spot in the UK singles chart, Marc's new label Fly released the first, eponymously titled *T. Rex* album. As much of an introduction to the new band profile as anything else, the album sounded like nothing recorded by them before. There was an excitement and vitality to the range of songs that was apparent from the moment the needle hit the vinyl. *NME*'s Nick Logan succinctly set the mood of the next few years: 'I don't know how much it is down to the great British public moving to meet Marc Bolan, or Marc Bolan moving to meet the great British public. But one thing "Ride a White Swan" and the new *T. Rex* album prove is that they have definitely met . . . [T]he album is the finest work the duo has presented to date.'

Wise words. I felt at the time, and still do, that each track had its own unique energy, paced beautifully; the lyrics had maturity about them and there was some of the best electric guitar work from Marc that I had heard to date. As a fan, I always believed that the fact that Marc Bolan was a self-taught guitarist gave him a freedom to play how he wanted and not how he *should*. The guitar work, the subtle little riffs, aggressive bursts – this was finally Marc Bolan stamping his authority on his music.

There were clever little moments throughout the LP. The teasing intro and outro, 'Children of Rarn', was a project that promised so much for the future; sadly, it saw the light of day only with Visconti's signature all over it, after Marc died. 'Jewel' bombards the senses with some pounding rhythmic drums pushing the Bolan vocals. The pace changes with the dreamy 'Diamond Meadows'. 'Is it Love', 'Beltane Walk' and

'One Inch Rock' are pure boogie rock and the remake of the 1965 single 'The Wizard' proves just how Marc had evolved musically. And the best was yet to come.

T. Rex retained the pixie-like innocence of both *Unicorn* and *A Beard of Stars*, but, much as a young child takes its first steps, demonstrated an innate understanding of how to survive and evolve towards adulthood; *T. Rex* was viewed by many as a debut LP. This was surely the music Bolan could easily have been producing immediately after his fleeting romance with John's Children.

The album, suggested Marc, was simply 'a selection of songs done for the first time as I really heard them'. The sounds in Marc's head became more dreamlike and emotional and as such only the use of orchestration could give full breadth to how Marc wanted the listener to join him on a journey. 'To me, strings are magical' Marc begins. 'They are old, and the wood has years and years of history. They are romantic . . .' When listening back to the album at first Marc panicked: 'God there are no lyrics. But of course, there are – these are people's words, like love songs.'

PART TWO

CATCH A BRIGHT STAR

FIERY LIPS ON IVORY HIPS AND THE EYES OF HILLY COUNTENANCE

A park where a horse lived and pastured
Like the eternal mother of the twisted mountain.
The evening gold rolled majestic
A cloud twig away from the deep steep, plays
The Damsel of Lay, pathed in emotion, the
Dreams of Syria furnish her heart
with down and gowns and feathers
To fly upon into the mist. And the Park is forever
God is together

From the published 2015 collection of poetry,
Marc Bolan – Natural Born Poet

1971

'Ride a White Swan' was No. 10 in the singles chart by 2 January 1971, while the *T. Rex* LP darted in and out of the album charts, eventually to peak at No. 7. By now, Marc's record company was starting to ask for a follow-up single, which Marc felt to be somewhat premature. After all, 'Ride a White Swan' still had life in it, having peaked at No. 2 on 23 January, and he was still tentative about going down the singles road again. Follow-ups, especially, had a nasty habit of kicking him in the teeth. Four years later, in 1975, Marc told *Sounds* journalist Geoff Barton, 'The only time I can remember getting really hurt was just after "Swan" broke. One paper wrote that it was "teenybopper trash", whereas in the previous week's edition I had been an underground hero. That, I couldn't quite get together in my head.'

In *The Record Producers*, Visconti discussed Marc Bolan and the evolution of T. Rex's classic line-up:

> After 'Ride a White Swan' we needed a drummer for 'Hot Love' and unlike Denny [Cordell] who used to get all the real slick session musicians like John McLaughlin, I tend to like guys who I can work with on a personality level. Their level of musicianship isn't too important, and much more important to me is the magic that can come from the right blend of personalities, and I know that I can make the right person sound great if I can just get on with him. At that time, the only drummer I was working with was Bill, who was with Legend, and I asked him if he'd like to play with Marc Bolan, and Bill said he'd love it.

'Marc was pretty relaxed,' Bill recalled when talking to me in 1991. 'He was sitting behind the desk and getting his sound together. We just shook hands – he was pretty friendly – and we really didn't hang around long, just went into the studio booth and started playing.' Of the other members of T. Rex: 'I didn't see [Mickey Finn] – no, that's not true: I suppose he was there but I was concentrating on the song itself, getting it together. I had obviously said hello to Steve Currie and I felt pretty much at home. The first tracks we recorded were "Hot Love" and "Woodland Rock", and the guys made it pretty easy to feel part of the setup.'

Steve Currie was already in the group as bass player, and recalls, 'Bill played on "Hot Love", and I think Marc offered him the permanent job that night. But Marc said, "I've got it

– we're not going to call you Bill Fifield" – which was his real name – "because that's not glamorous enough. We're going to call you Bill Legend, because you came from a group called Legend." And that was how Legend lost a drummer, and T. Rex gained one.'

At the end of the 'Hot Love' recording session, Marc was indeed impressed enough with Bill to offer him a full-time place in the band. With his arrival, the first T. Rex line-up was complete.

'Hot Love' was released on 19 February 1971, to rave reviews. Whereas 'Ride a White Swan' was an up-tempo but basic-sounding track, incorporating just electric guitar, bass and strings, 'Hot Love' was a laid-back, dreamy affair, with a full rhythm section. One reviewer noted that, 'Although still doing very well with "Ride a White Swan", T. Rex has elected to rush out this new disc . . . The very simplicity of the number is the key to its assured popularity.'

Bolan himself told *ZigZag*: '"Hot Love" I wrote because I wanted to write a rock record – I know it's exactly like a million other songs, but I hope it's got a little touch of me in it too. It was done as a happy record, I wanted to make a 12-bar a hit. What happened was we got very lushed one night, had four bottles of brandy, it was about four in the morning, and we just did it.' He also claimed to have written it in just ten minutes.

Disc and Music Echo wrote of the song that it was 'more of an old-time rock-n-roll beat with shades of "All Shook Up" among others . . . I love it! For the record, "Woodland Rock" on the other side is another rock-n-roll spoof, this time based on "Long Tall Sally" and her ilk.' Marc explained to the music press that 'Hot Love' was 'cosmic rock . . . it's not how I remember a 1950s rock record, but how I wanted to do it now and features Howard Kaylan and Mark Volman from the Mothers, in their regular role as our backing vocalists.'

T. Rex completed the first leg of their British tour at Nottingham University on 20 February 1971, the day after the release of 'Hot Love'. Marc was finally a rock-'n'-roll sensation. The first week of March was spent on a whirlwind tour of Ireland, during which the band appeared in Cork, Belfast and Dublin on consecutive days. Then, back on the mainland, T. Rex did what proved to be the last of the university-style gigs to packed houses. The problems with security had become insurmountable due to the exponential increase in the band's popularity, and Bolan himself felt very much at risk. Amazingly, during this month Fly took what seemed a backward step in the band's promotion by planning the release of a 'best of' compilation. There was only one possible explanation for this: money. The album itself was part of a series of back-catalogue releases by Fly (also including compilations by the Move and Procol Harum) and was advertised as containing two previously unreleased tracks, 'Blessed Wild Apple Girl' and the mystical 'Once Upon the Seas of Abyssinia'. All the tracks were Tyrannosaurus Rex tracks. The rather crass exploitation of rock's new phenomenon was nothing new and, of course, putting the T. Rex brand name on something (as many people did) guaranteed a healthy bank balance. That said, at £1, and as a teenager, I thought 'Job done!' In the UK, 'Hot Love' spent the whole of April 1971 holding the No. 1 position, while T. Rex were on tour in America.

It must have been quite frustrating for Marc to play to audiences Stateside who were still not truly switched on to the T. Rex sound. None of this was helped by the fact that, back at home, he was now a rock star in the ascendancy, whereas in the States his star barely shimmered. On returning to England, the clamour for the band to perform live intensified. Demand to see this new pop phenomenon had escalated to the point at which only major city halls could accommodate his huge number of fans. Marc again insisted that ticket prices on the new tour, which began on 9 May at the Bournemouth Winter Gardens, should be pegged at 60p. However, it was neither the price of a ticket nor the fact that the new tour started there that was to put Bournemouth on the map. It was the fans.

During the day of the first gig in Bournemouth, there were scenes more reminiscent of a football crowd making their way to a ground than a concert audience. Along with a group of friends, I milled around chatting with previously unknown groups of Bolan teenagers, wearing scarves around their necks and wrists in yellows, blues and whites, all bearing the same circular photos of our hero, with the words 'Marc Bolan' on one side and 'T. Rex' on the other.

It was a fantastic feeling to be among similar-minded youngsters. Inside the hall, there was a very strange, almost intimidating atmosphere; an electrical tension. Surely even Marc, in his heart of hearts, could not possibly have been ready for the effect he had on the audience when he and the band first stepped on stage. Girls simply jumped from their seats and dashed towards them, building up a solid wall of screaming teenagers who began to claw themselves closer to the new messiah. So single-minded were they in their efforts that they tore at each other's clothes and ripped at flesh. Nothing mattered but to get as close as they could. Fans further back, myself included, stood no chance of seeing the band; we simply looked at each other and resigned ourselves to taking a back seat to the events unfolding before us. The scenes were to be repeated throughout the other thirteen dates of the three-week tour.

On 25 June, the music press announced that a new T. Rex single was to be rush-released on Friday of the following week. 'Get It On' had been recorded in Los Angeles during the most recent tour of America. Backing vocals were supplied once more by Kaylan and Volman, with the addition of Ian McDonald, formerly saxophonist with King Crimson. Many predicted that the new single was already guaranteed the top spot: 'Even if T. Rex changed their name to protect the innocent . . . it's just instantly commercial . . . an excellent sense of rhythm and power . . . an instant basic riff which clicks even after a couple of bars . . . it's instant and it's a giant hit,' cooed one uncredited review. At this juncture two new live dates were also to be added, at the Birmingham Odeon on 2 July and London's Lewisham Odeon on 9 July; these were the last dates before the next full tour in the autumn.

'Get It On' took just two weeks to hit the top spot in the singles chart and give Marc his second No. 1 in the space of four months. Technically, it contained not two but three flipsides, with 'Raw Ramp', 'There Was a Time' and 'Electric Boogie'. 'Get It On' 'was initially going to be either "Sweet Little Sixteen" or "Little Queenie"', Marc later revealed, explaining that he had planned to record one of the above but, after spending time rehearsing and laying down demo tracks, his mind kept returning to 'Get It On'.

There was something special about 'Get It On' – the vibe had a raunchy feel to it but at the same time a very laid-back groove that, as a fan, I found intoxicating. Listening to Marc evolve with each new release was an astonishing experience. While researching various articles and in-depth interviews with Marc, I stumbled upon the following uncredited piece, in which he shone a light on his writing style, in his own unique way.

When I start a song, I work it out acoustically. Then I play it with a band and it changes. When you're playing on your own you're totally free, right? It's your own universe. When you get other people in you have to get some sort of beat going for the people to relate to and that's where the song changes, always, because drummers can't always play what you want, and you don't necessarily know what you want. I hear the songs with a rock band and put my voice on and then see what it needs more. Then I'll get whoever's around at the time or get anyone depending on what I want. If I want a sax, I'll get someone like that. Whoever's around. I'll always get the best people, but I never know until it's almost finished. I don't use studio employees. I used friends. I get them in the studio and play the song for about an hour and then put them on so I get the flavour of how they see it.

The more successful the band became, the more security was needed. It got to a stage where just getting the short distance from the stage door to the cars meant taking their lives in their hands. Once they were outside, girls would simply launch themselves at the cars, climbing onto the roofs. The most unnerving episodes occurred when they hammered on the windows and could be heard scratching away on the roof, trying desperately to get at Marc and Mickey.

June Feld went everywhere with Marc 'I know it sounds silly but it really got very scary,' Marc admitted. It was a level of fan mania not seen since the days of the Beatles and the Rolling Stones in the 1960s.

I went to the Lewisham gig on 9 July and experienced the scale of this fan obsession at first hand. As our small group approached, we could hear chanting of Marc's name and the occasional female squeal. It felt as if the walls were shaking.

The whole evening was a demonstration of the magic that line-up held. Once you were in, it was a question of where best to be when Marc and the band emerged. Previous encounters taught me to take cover when Marc appeared. Eventually, he ran across the stage and proceeded to deliver an amazing guitar solo, using pedals, feedback and an astounding wall of reverb. Mickey, Bill and Steve then appeared as Marc kicked in for a heavy rendition of 'One Inch Rock', before changing tempo with a beautiful version of 'Girl', sitting cross legged on the stage with an acoustic guitar as accompaniment. 'Deborah' followed, with Mickey Finn on bongos. The band back in place, the house rocked to the sounds of 'Ride a White Swan', 'Hot Love' and 'Get It On'.

The band, having whipped up the audience into a frenzy, then disappeared, waving and throwing mementos as they left. But nobody in the crowd started to turn away towards the exits. Instead, as one, we began chanting, 'Bolan, Bolan, Bolan!' After what seemed an eternity, fans started screaming as, one by one, T. Rex reappeared in front of an adoring crowd and proceeded to play the only non-Bolan song of the evening – 'Summertime Blues', the Eddie Cochrane classic.

It having finally dawned on me that the band were not going to reappear, we grudgingly decided it was time to return to reality and go home. It always amazed me how high I felt after a T. Rex gig. There were always mixed emotions, not to mention the physical effect that usually meant a headache, a buzzing in the ears, and complete physical draining. Would I have changed these experiences? Did I learn anything from these nights? Clearly not, as I returned time and time again to pay homage to the Master.

There were four gigs in August, culminating with T. Rex's appearance at the Weeley Festival, one of those three-day-event specialities that had originally surfaced during the 1960s. On a hot August Bank Holiday weekend, the acts that appeared alongside T. Rex included Barclay James Harvest, King Crimson, the Faces and Lindisfarne. Not that everyone who attended cared for T. Rex. Certain sections of the audience seemed intent on chastising Bolan and the band for the unforgivable digression of becoming popular. True, Marc hardly helped his cause by announcing as he appeared on stage, 'I'm Marc Bolan – you've seen me on *Top of the Pops* – I'm a big star.' Further abuse ensued until Marc himself retorted, 'Why don't you fuck off . . . If you don't want to listen then I'll leave.' Once Marc let his music do the talking, however, the crowd reaction changed for the better.

Interestingly, the set included several songs that were

to appear on *The Slider* and single flipsides nearly two years later. Opening the set with 'Cadillac', the band then performed 'One Inch Rock' followed by acoustic renditions of 'Spaceball Ricochet', 'Girl' and 'Debora', performed cross-legged on the stage. With the old school of fans satisfied, the tempo increased to the new high-octane T. Rex: 'Ride a White Swan', 'Hot Love' and 'Get It On' stood out from the set. One review suggested, 'You can't compare either Bolan or T. Rex to other bands, they are a power unto themselves and an essence that needs savouring on more than one hearing and under far better conditions than at Weeley.'

September could have been classed as slow, except for the fact that on the 17th of the month the most significant and enduring T. Rex album of all was released. Ironically, it was both the first No. 1 T. Rex album and the last LP on the Fly label. *Electric Warrior* was easily the most impressive long-player by the band, and on so many different levels. All the ingredients were there: romance, blues, mythology and good old rock 'n' roll. There was another special ingredient: the fun factor. It was clearly audible that a great time had been had by everyone involved. Moreover, it was performed with supreme confidence. '*Electric Warrior* was made to be danceable,' declared a very proud Marc at the time. If he had been able to blueprint his career, he could not have planned it better. He was in demand – red hot. As far as his musical career and recording future were concerned, he could now name his own price.

It is difficult, at times, to put into words the buzz of euphoria when a new album from Marc Bolan was forthcoming. The days of simply connecting to iTunes, Spotify and Amazon

Music and downloading were way in the future. I remember often going down to my local record store and pleading with the assistant behind the counter to play me a couple of tracks.

When the stunning *Electric Warrior* was released – an album that I considered to be the finest collection of songs Marc could possibly have put together – I enjoyed only limited pocket money, so I was over the proverbial 'bebop moon' when my aunt Dee announced that she was going to London for a few days, then asked whether there was anything I would like her to bring back. *Electric Warrior*, please, by T. Rex!

Although somewhat fazed by the title, let alone the name of the band, my aunt refused to visit just any record store – that was too working-class. So, while shopping in a posh department store, she found herself staring at a massive display of record covers and posters for the new T. Rex album. When she returned that night, she handed over a bag emblazoned with the word 'Harrods' and within this bag was my album – shrink-wrapped and bearing a red oblong sticker that stated 'free poster'.

Bolan was always keen to provide his fans with a little bit extra: 'I like to be able to give away something that the kids would have otherwise had to go out and buy,' he once told Steve Turner, of *Beat Instrumentals*. 'I want to be able to use my position to contribute back to people – I'm one of the people too, you know. I was the first person to put a give-away lyric sheet with the album *My People Were Fair*, and Tyrannosaurus Rex albums. I'd dig to give away free badges as well – if you've got a hole in your trousers, I'd rather be the one to give you something to sew on it.'

Whichever way you want to look at it, *Electric Warrior* was undoubtedly a landmark achievement in Bolan's career, both as performer and producer. As an innocent teenager I always assumed that Marc Bolan and T. Rex simply disappeared into a studio, sang into microphones, plugged instruments into God knows what and that was it, done and dusted. All these years later – and having had the good fortune, in the eighties and nineties, to locate a great many T. Rex multitrack tapes – I now know differently. (Seven of the eleven tracks were recorded in the USA, either in New York or at Wally Heider's San Francisco studios. The remaining four tracks were made in London.)

In October 1971, T. Rex began their Electric Warrior tour, their second major UK tour of the year. It was a sellout and took in a gruelling seventeen dates in little over three weeks. Starting at the Portsmouth Guildhall on 19 October, the tour should have ended at the Wigan ABC on 10 November. However, such had been the demand that T. Rex swiftly moved on to the Liverpool Stadium for two shows on 11 November.

Bolan had more than the tour to occupy his thoughts, though. His recording contract with Fly was about to come to an end. At this stage, he had acquired the advisory services of Tony Secunda to help him to negotiate a new deal. Secunda had been involved with a string of successful acts, as either an adviser or a manager: Johnny Kidd and the Pirates, the Moody Blues, Procol Harum and the Move. He also introduced guitarist Mick Taylor to the Rolling Stones, the band having asked Brian Jones to leave in June 1969 (less than a month later, Jones drowned in his swimming pool). Secunda had managed

Alan White, previously with John Lennon and Yoko Ono's Plastic Ono Band and Yes.

A major contributor to the formation of Blind Faith, one of the world's first supergroups, the versatile Secunda also represented Denny Laine, originally with the Moody Blues, who then went on to join Paul and Linda McCartney's Wings. Marc Bolan had hired a man who was known to be a sharp operator, something of a Svengali figure and a tough negotiator; he ticked all the right boxes. Little did the wider world know that, rather than being just another artist on someone else's record label, Marc was aiming to assume full control of his recording career.

It was *Melody Maker* that disclosed Marc Bolan's plan to form his own record label, following in the footsteps of the Beatles, the Rolling Stones and the Moody Blues. Exalted company indeed. Regal Zonophone and Fly were both distributed by EMI, which put together a package that would, they felt, keep Marc 'extremely happy'. Marc told *Melody Maker*, 'The label situation is that we haven't done a deal yet. We are having a meeting now to suss that very question. It is very possible that I may have my own label. I want to do that and I want the best quality product at the best prices. I would like to record other artistes very much too.'

It would be pure speculation to guess as to whether Marc would have stayed with Fly had circumstances been different. That said, his displeasure at the release of his 'new' single was certainly well documented at the time. I asked June Feld about this: 'Was there any truth in the rumour that Marc was thoroughly pissed off with Fly for releasing "Jeepster" when, in fact, it was never meant to be a single?' 'No,' she replied, 'he loved "Jeepster".' The song was lifted from the *Electric Warrior* album and backed with another track from the album, 'Life's a Gas' – but it was never intended as an official single. It surfaced as a limited-edition, special-preview, seven-inch disc and was simply meant to be a special thank-you by T. Rex to everyone in the business who had supported them throughout 1971.

June continued, 'I mean – it was a really good song. And the truth of the matter was that Marc . . . wrote "Jeepster" many, many years before and had signed it away to . . . one of these nebulous [laughs] people that just came out of the woodwork after "Debora". They suddenly appeared claiming all this money. But . . . Essex owned [all of his publishing] and one of the songs was "Jeepster". And then this man came and said, "I've got a piece of paper signed by Marc's mum, Mrs Phyllis Feld" . . . that gave him the rights to "Jeepster". So, there was all that kerfuffle going on. Anyway, after all that settled down, Essex [the music publishers] and David Platz decided to pay the man off.'

That said, June recalled, '[Marc] was very cross when they put them out and it always seemed to coincide with things that EMI and Marc had planned for their releases. But for me that's dog eat dog and that's what the music business is about [. . .] the bigger the dog and the better your teeth. You win. Or you [laughs] – or you get muzzled.'

'Jeepster' was released on 1 November and by the last week of that same month it occupied the No. 2 position in the UK singles chart behind the band who, at the time, were Marc's closest rivals – Slade, with 'Coz I Luv You'. Except for the first week's chart of December, when 'Jeepster' slipped to No.

3, T. Rex spent the remainder of 1971 at No. 2. Which rock band or artist kept Marc from his third successive No. 1? Was it Tom Jones? Was it the Carpenters? Was it Cliff Richard? Slade or Status Quo? No, it was comedian Benny Hill with a little ditty called 'Ernie (the Fastest Milkman in the West)'.

The year 1971 had seen the birth of an Electric Warrior in the shape of Marc Bolan. T. Rex had two bestselling singles in the 1971 Top Ten listings, the only act to do so that year. *Electric Warrior* was ranked the fifth-best-selling album of 1971 and, not surprisingly, T. Rex were handed the top accolade of best band of 1971 by *NME*, a verdict determined by assessing weekly chart positions over the year. T. Rex amassed a respectable 980 points. Radio Luxembourg, in its debut shot at handing out plaudits to British artists who have made 'major contributions to the music industry', credited T. Rex and 'Ride a White Swan' with the group performance of the year.

JOHN & TONY SMITH PRESENT

SAT. 18th. MARCH

ADDITIONAL SHOW at 5.30pm

& Now SOLD OUT!

TICKETS 75p.

T. REX

LIVE AT WEMBLEY

PLUS!
QUIVER
EMPEROR ROSKO
HEAVYLIGHTS

BEING FILMED
FOR POSTERITY!!

TICKETS AVAILABLE FROM
ALL HARLEQUIN RECORD SHOPS.
POSTAL APPLICATION TO:
HARLEQUIN RECORDS,
67 GT. TITCHFIELD ST., W.1.
Postal Orders & S.A.E. ONLY

1972

'The prospect of being immortal doesn't excite me, but the prospect of being a materialistic idol for four years does appeal.'
MARC BOLAN

For Marc Bolan and T. Rex, the year 1972 started as 1971 had finished: with panache and a glittering promise of further domination of the music charts. Months of speculation over the band's new recording contract and label deal finally ended on Monday, 3 January, when Bolan announced the formation of his own record label, the T. Rex Wax Co. For its part, EMI was also delighted with the arrangement, as T. Rex would continue to be distributed by it. In an interview with June Feld in 1991, I asked her about the reasons behind Marc's leaving Fly. She replied, quite frankly, 'Ego. The Rolling Stones had their own record label . . . all his peer-group rock-and-rollers, who also had tremendously much more money than Marc ever did . . . had their own things going for them – their own publishing companies . . . [so] he wanted his own, albeit as a distribution under . . . the umbrella of EMI – but it was his own and it had his picture on the label . . . and it made him very happy at the time.'

That the debut T. Rex Wax Co. offering of 1972 would be a hit was a safe bet. However, even EMI were reportedly staggered when advance orders ensured a release-day figure more than 90,000 copies. The following week, as 'Jeepster' disappeared from the singles chart, 'Telegram Sam', backed with 'Cadillac' and 'Baby Strange', entered at No. 3, the band's highest-ever first-week placing. Reviewer Chris Welch began his assessment of the track by acknowledging, 'Like all T. Rex singles, by the third play you get it on. At first hearing one tends to say, "Gosh, chaps, Marc's new single sounds a bit of an oldie." [But] press the headphones a little closer and one begins to convulse in a not altogether unpleasant fashion . . . Boley piles on the guitar riff and the strings topple around him with rocking menace. According to Beep [B P Fallon], Marc's famous representative, "'Telegram Sam' is all of us".' Another breathless reviewer gushed: 'Nothing more or less than a good old-fashioned stomping rocker, given the stamp of individuality by Bolan's own peculiarly distinctive vocal delivery . . . Beaty, compelling, insistent and catchy.'

T. Rex did only one gig in England during January – at Boston's Starlight Club in Lincolnshire (15th). A crowd more than five thousand strong materialised from all parts of the UK. Courtesy of James Johnson, *NME* summed it all up in the headline 'Rexmania'. Johnson observed, 'On Saturday, T. Rex turned the musical clock back to the early sixties. In scenes of hysteria and confusion unparalleled since the days of Beatlemania, thirty-three people fainted and one girl was taken to hospital after falling off the balcony in her excitement.' He went on to set the scene:

> There's tension in the air. Crash barriers have been erected around the stage, bouncers nervously sip cans of beer trying to look tough for the chicks and a television crew try to act cool hampered all the time by people jostling for a good position . . . Bolan stands out front pouting to the front-line of out-stretched hands trying to touch anything connected with the group . . . Finn frighteningly stone-faced, rushes across the stage whipping the crowd up into all kinds of frenzies whilst the bassist and drummer plug away expressionlessly churning out the rhythm.

On the chart published for the week commencing 2 February, T. Rex had done it again. The coveted No. 1 position was theirs for the third time in four attempts. Not that they were in England to celebrate: they were touring in America, where they would stay for most of the month. But the celebrations would not have lasted long, in any case, as the top spot in the UK charts was theirs for a mere two weeks before 'Son of My Father' by Chicory Tip knocked them into second place. There they stayed for the remainder of the month.

During this time, rumours circulated that Marc Bolan and T. Rex were to retire altogether from touring. This had some grounding in truth: Marc was finding it increasingly difficult to handle the reactions of his British fans; the horrendous problems of security, it appeared, were his chief concern. Although America did not generate fears for his personal safety, it provided its own challenges for T. Rex: the country was nowhere near as easy to crack as England. While Marc was chalking up a third No. 1 back home, the Americans remained, largely, uninterested. The seven-venue tour of the States had kicked off in Hollywood on 15 February ending at New York's Carnegie Hall on 27 February. It was following this last gig that Secunda and Bolan were to part company.

Bolan was apparently unhappy with the American audience's reactions to the band (the crowds had reportedly preferred Uriah Heap, the support band). Moreover, he had appeared on stage at Carnegie Hall the worse for wear from drink, falling over on stage as he played the first number in the set.

On returning to England, T. Rex carried on where they'd left off. It was announced that they would be appearing at Wembley's Empire Pool in London on Saturday, 18 March. The ticket price was 75p and the gig sold out within days, which was hardly surprising considering all the uncertainty around whether T. Rex would tour again. What's more, it was the only UK date to be announced in the press that year. As it turned out, the concert was an extra-special occasion, with the afternoon and evening performances filmed by ex-Beatle drummer turned film director Ringo Starr, for a documentary to be released by Apple Films sometime in the future. It was a magical day and, for the twenty thousand fans who were lucky enough to be there, either during the afternoon matinée performance or for the evening show, its memory will live on for ever. 'Bolan's triumph' and 'Twenty thousand screamers and the day that pop came back' screamed the headlines in the music press. There was another headline, though, that summed it all up: 'Monster power!'

I remember those two gigs with a unique affection. Other gigs over the years have undoubtedly been fun, euphoric and ear-deafening, but I will never forget the day twenty thousand screamers came to Wembley. For me at least, the scenes outside the Empire Pool that day were no different from those usually associated with gatherings in another part of Wembley – for FA Cup finals and England football internationals. Outside the venue, ticket touts were asking £4 and £5 for a 75p ticket. Unofficial programmes, posters and scarves were on sale everywhere and eager fans paid over the odds for anything, wanting to grasp everything on offer (they were not aware, at that point, that official merchandise was on sale inside the complex). Personally, I found what little merchandise there was to be less than inspiring.

All around, groups of people were gabbling excitedly, a sea of teenage faces witnessing a thousand Christmases all rolled into one. As we were ushered like cattle through doorways into the main hall, our first impressions were of a vast tiered galaxy of seats, row upon row of them. Looking skywards, we could see other constellations of fans seeming to move around the heavens as the lights from the ceiling of the complex twinkled like small, isolated stars. The gangways stretched ahead and in the distance, at the front of the auditorium, was what seemed to be a tiny stage. Was the whole band really going to fit on that?

As we moved forward to find our seats, the backdrop images of Marc became clearer, as did a huge cardboard cutout of him on the right-hand side of the arena. Fans walked tentatively towards their seats, and suddenly there was an ocean of Bolan lookalikes all around. The audience bobbed up and down like swimmers in a strong sea. They were nervous with excitement, trying to decide whether to sit down or stand up for a better view. The support band, Quiver, came on stage first – an appropriate name for anyone who had to play first to an audience who really were not at all interested in them. This turned out to be an especially unfair assessment of their talents, though, as they performed well. As their set finished and the applause died away, there was a new tension of expectation: the Wizard himself would soon grace the stage with his presence. Emperor Rosko, a popular DJ at the time, was doing his best to keep the crowd entertained by playing records, when suddenly the whole atmosphere changed and the chants of Marc's name got louder and louder.

'It's star time . . . they're just back from a coast-to-coast tour of America . . . it's—' The rest of the Emperor's introduction was drowned out in a blast of cheering, screaming voices. Bill Legend and Steve Currie were first in view, followed shortly afterwards by Mickey Finn, who waved as screams greeted him; and then, in that split second of time when the audience shiver from the emotion of it all, Marc, the main man, appeared on stage. Over an hour of music followed, none of which I can remember with any clarity. The fans must have wondered if they would survive the experience at all as they withstood the breathless crush of the crowd and felt the urge to panic. But Bolan's performance proved mesmerising and a distraction from such fears; they followed his every move. At one point, miniature tambourines were thrown into the audience, causing another surge forward as those at the back realised that only those nearer the front stood a chance of catching one.

I managed finally to catch one of these gifts from the Messiah in my hands, only to succumb to the glances of a beautiful girl with a glitter-dusted face pleading to hand it over to her. I rejoined the pack and could not believe my luck when another tambourine, launched from my idol's own hand – as if in slow motion – landed in outstretched palms. 'Thanks, Marc,' I silently mouthed, believing that Bolan had personally witnessed my earlier act of chivalry. To my left, another face looked pained and hopeful, but getting the first was lucky; the second came direct from Marc, and this time I hung on to my prize, not pushing my luck for a possible third gift. (A couple of years after that gig I rashly did what I refused to do that day. I gave my cherished tambourine away to a girlfriend and I have regretted it ever since.)

Suddenly it was all over. Marc waved and disappeared from sight. But the fans could not believe it and the chanting started up again, telling the band not to leave without at least one more glimpse. After what felt like an eternity, T. Rex came back on stage to launch into 'Summertime Blues', the Cochran rock-'n'-roll classic. Then it really was all over and slowly the huge audience left the complex. Finally we could catch our breath and take stock of what we had all just experienced – the togetherness, the uniqueness of the occasion as something to relish for ever.

Marc was interviewed later by Steve Peacock for *Sounds*. During the interview, he was asked how it felt to be on stage, and be aware that a vast auditorium of people were focused on him, their idol. 'I'm more concerned about whether my guitar's in tune, to be honest,' he responded. 'There's too much to think about on stage because I know that if I stop playing, or if no one plays for ten minutes, the whole thing will be a shambles. So, you try to keep the motion of the show together.'

Marc was then asked whether he realised just how seriously the kids took him: to Marc it may be just a 'jive'; to the kids, though, it's much more. He replied, 'It's nothing to do with me. I'm what I am and I can't change what I am. I do what I do, and I respond – it's all the same thing, it's one. Without them, I'm just a poet. With them I'm a rock and roll star – trophies man, like rhinoceros' heads. I didn't shoot them though. I didn't shoot the rhinoceros. That's the difference.'

In a similar vein, Marc defended himself to Keith Altham in September 1972: 'I suppose I'm a sort of teenage idol but I'm not a teeny-bop idol. What people do with you in their own minds you can't stop, but I think of myself as an idol only in the same way that George Harrison once was, and I'd be very upset if the press wrote me off as anything less than a musician and a poet.' He went on to add:

If there's going to be any kind of revolution in pop music, it must come from young people. If you ignore them, you're cutting yourself off from the life force of rock music. I've done quite a few interviews for so called teen-magazines and I've very seldom been asked a stupid question. Most young people know what it's all about, intuitively.

I have a right to go on stage and do what I want, and the public has the right not to listen, or not come and watch – but if they come and have a go at me they can expect the back lash of my tongue or a guitar on their head . . . It gets very difficult to take critics seriously, though, when you discover, as I did recently, that two reviews of my concert appeared in two different papers – one was a slagging-off, and the other high praise – written by the same man under different names!'

This, concerning the difference between the fans who drink in every moment at a gig and those who want to ridicule him, might have struck a chord with regular attenders at Marc's gigs. I remember on more than one occasion finding myself standing next to, it must be said, men with no interest in Marc Bolan whatsoever. The irony is that they were usually accompanied by females bedecked in Bolan regalia, and one can therefore only assume they were at the gig under duress.

In the same week in which all the papers were full of heady reviews of the Empire Pool gig, Fly started to reissue a batch of old releases, much to the displeasure of the singer himself. The initial reissue was the very first Tyrannosaurus Rex single, 'Debora', released as part of a maxi single containing three other Tyrannosaurus Rex titles: 'One Inch Rock', 'Woodland Bop' and 'The Seal of Seasons'. It eventually peaked at No. 7 in the singles chart. It might seem like something of a contradiction for Marc to be so against its release – after all, as Fly rightly commented, he was earning royalties on the hit. There was, however, a real conflict of interest within Marc himself. His problem really centred on the musical development of the band. It is highly likely that he was struggling with the fact that the reissues were ancient history and did not represent where he now wanted T. Rex to be seen musically.

When asked for his reaction to the release of 'Debora', he

gave the following reply to *Melody Maker* on 29 April: 'I'd like to make the point that it's nothing to do with me. They're obviously going to keep putting those records out, so I've been told. Of course, they are. They've got a lot of product. They've got five other ones that we probably know the titles of, which would be potentially biggies now.'

Melody Maker pointed out that Fly had maintained it would have been impossible to release them without Bolan's permission. He replied, 'I know. Legally, that's what they told me. Legally that's true. Meanwhile, I think 'Debora' is at number five [*sic*] now. In five records' time, I'd probably take out an injunction against them. But I just don't wanna do all that. That's the last thing the kids need. We'll squash them with the new one in five minutes. I just wish I had it ready sooner so I could put it out the second week and squash them altogether.'

Following these remarks, Bolan received an open letter from Fly records, signed by label manager David Ruffell:

Your comments in last week's press struck us as being a little odd, to say the least, and we would like the chance to clear up several points. The record was issued, not on the regular Fly label, but as one of a series of, initially four, Magni Flys intended to make available again classic recordings in maxi single form. It was never promoted as the follow-up to 'Telegram Sam' and we even took the trouble to put the series out in a special sleeve with photographs taken from around the time of the original release. Even the label says Tyrannosaurus Rex and not T. Rex.

You also say that 'Debora' is unrepresentative of what you are doing now, but when we saw you not so long ago you were still performing it acoustically and better than ever. Own up, Marc, 'Debora' was great then and always will be. If your fans want to buy it on a single with three other tracks, then surely that's their right. Keep bopping.

The reissue of 'Debora' clearly rankled with Bolan a great deal. Yet, when Fly released the first two Tyrannosaurus Rex albums as a double pack, not a word was heard from him. Within four weeks it held the No. 1 slot in the album charts.

During April, while the Tyrannosaurus Rex reissues were soaring up the album charts, London Weekend Television screened an episode in its series *Music in the Round*, previously recorded on 8 December 1971. T. Rex performed live, without the aid of backing tracks, to a selected studio audience. They blasted through 'Telegram Sam', 'Cadillac', 'Jeepster' and an amazing version of 'Spaceball Ricochet'. It was an all-too-rare occurrence, but one well worth the effort. Marc was at his most relaxed when he was interviewed by Humphrey Burton between songs and handled the occasion well. It was clear that Burton had no idea how to deal with Bolan, though, and obviously did not understand what all the fuss was about.

Burton kicked off the interview after T. Rex had opened the set with 'Jeepster': 'Is "Jeepster", by any stretch of the imagination rock – or is it something different?' he asked. Marc responded, 'It's seventies rock – as opposed to the earlier stuff. The earlier stuff was great, but the recordings were basic.'

Burton then went on to ask Marc about the song 'Cadillac': 'I noticed that a lot of your songs are about cars – are cars important?' 'Yes,' replied Marc, who went on to expand on the subject. 'I've got an American Cadillac, given to me by a friend; it's a work of art. I don't drive, but it's an incredible piece of art.'

'A lot of people', Burton then observed, 'have criticised your kind of music – my generation and beyond – for being too loud. You don't think that, obviously?' Marc explains, 'It's kind of an expression – it's an art form where you use volume to express yourself. Volume allows you to get more into the music.' 'Yes,' conceded Burton, 'but many people are saying the music is monotonous and that it is only loud.' Marc's face clouded over; he was obviously a little put out. 'A lot of people say a lot of things about a lot of stuff,' he snapped. 'You know many of them are not well informed on what they're talking about! Rock music is easily as important as any other music. Music is a thing one feels about and enjoys and, if one does not feel and enjoy, then one shouldn't talk about it – or listen to it.'

Burton was obviously enjoying Marc's reaction as he continued, 'So what do you mean by more important? Do you mean a lot more people get pleasure and excitement out of this than any other kind of music?' 'Yeah,' Marc confirms, 'as a kid I hated classical music.' The subject then moves on to the 100-watt speakers towering in the background during the interview. 'Why', asks Burton, 'do you have these huge loudspeakers?' Marc becomes relaxed again as he answers, 'Well, basically, most of the halls we play in are very big, consequently you would not hear us at the back.' 'How big are your audiences?' Burton asks. 'Normally around five thousand,' Marc proudly replies. Burton is stunned: 'Five thousand! Well we've only got about fifteen hundred in here – so this is—' And, before he could go on, Marc interrupted him with, 'This is a small room.'

Not to be denied, Burton returned to the volume trail. 'But then when you've got that enormous big sound—' Marc interrupted again, slightly exasperated: 'Yeah, but in a hall you're playing it's not always necessarily very loud.' 'Comfortable?' asks Burton. 'Yeah – comfortable,' agrees Marc.

Burton then moved on to the lyrics of Marc's songs and began by quoting from the acoustic number Marc had just performed, 'Spaceball Ricochet': 'It's a real poem that rhymes – not simply like the earlier songs?' 'No, lyrically,' Marc replied, 'it's probably one of the most important songs I've written.' 'Were you influenced by any poets? There are many rich words in your book *The Warlock of Love* – where did you gather them from?' Marc looked seriously at Burton. 'I don't really know – I believe I was, in a previous life, some kind of bard. Most of the things I write about are descriptions of places I've obviously never been to and most of the words I write you won't find in any dictionary anywhere and' – Marc owned up with a smile – 'I spell appallingly.'

Burton then invited questions from the audience. A young girl asked, 'Do you get more satisfaction out of writing poetry or singing songs?' Marc smiled and responded with, 'If I'm pleased with a poem I'm satisfied; if I'm pleased with a song I'm satisfied – there's really no difference. Many people say why don't you make music like you used to? I think I am – I only make what I wanted to play.'

Another young girl then asked which group of people Marc thought he appealed to most – just the young girls, or lots of different groups of people? 'There are not just young girls here,' Marc observed. Burton interjects, 'They are mostly young girls – come on, Marc, let's not get away from the fact. I'd say they were 90 per cent. I'm not saying anything against them – it's very nice!' 'I hope that anyone who takes their music seriously takes me seriously,' Marc interjected. 'People I work with. There is a mutual respect and artistically that's all I can ask for.'

The reviews that followed the show were scathing about Burton and his interview. The following reflects how one unaccredited reviewer saw the show pan out:

Marc Bolan's appearance on London Weekend Television's *Music in the Round* was embarrassing through no fault of his own. The interviewer, Humphrey Burton, was obviously totally at a loss for constructive comment or discussion, his script was appalling and his discomfort blatantly apparent. Bolan did his best with the inane questions, but the flat atmosphere of the studios couldn't have helped. The audience looked as though they couldn't have cared less about the band and could have been watching the Epilogue for all the interest they showed in the music. The entire show looked very third rate and shoddy, the only bright spots being the actual music. And as Marc referred to 'Telegram Sam' being their possible new single, it shows how long ago it was recorded, too. Bolan deserves better.

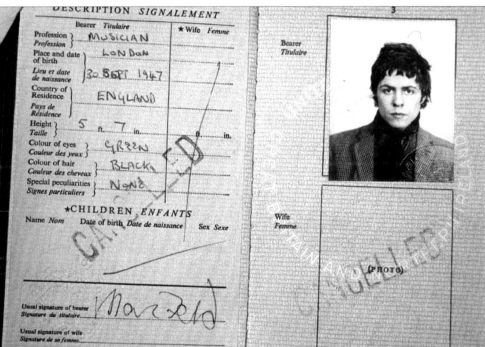

Above: An eighteen-year-old Marc, pictured in London in 1965, after the release of his first single, 'The Wizard'.

Below: Marc Bolan's passport from his 1967 tour (notice his rather dubious claim to being five feet and seven inches tall!). The passport was later auctioned at Christie's in London.

Tyrannosaurus Rex, comprised of Steve Peregrin Took and Marc Bolan, perform in Hyde Park in 1968.

Above: Marc Bolan relishing the bright lights of the television stage.

© *Michael Ochs/Getty*

Below: T. Rex perform on *Top of the Pops* in 1970 (*left to right*: Steve Currie, Marc Bolan and Mickey Finn).

© *Redferns/Getty Images*

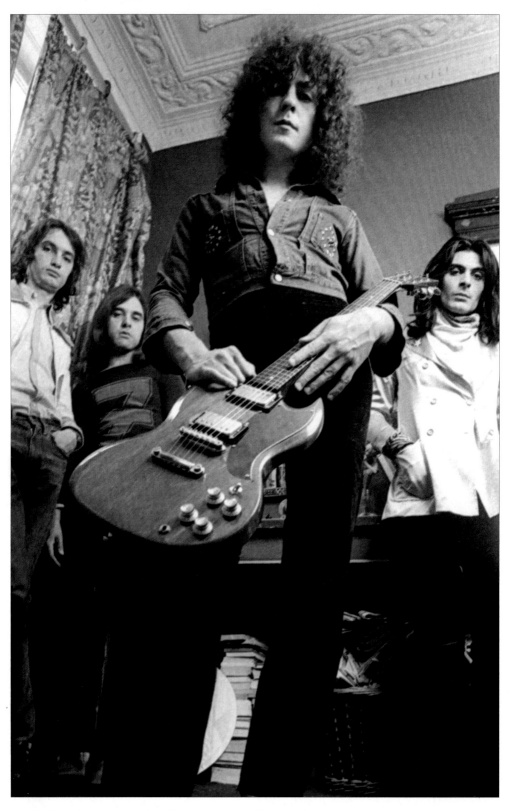

A 1971 band shot, featuring Steve Currie, Bill Legend, Marc Bolan (complete with devil-horned Gibson SG) and Mickey Finn.

© Michael Putland/Getty

Mickey Finn's handsome, aquiline features were essential to T. Rex's image – and the perfect foil for Marc's natural shimmer and sparkle.

© Araldo Di Crollazanza/Rex

Bottom left: T. Rex on Top of the Pops performing 'Ride a White Swan'. Note rare picture of Mickey Finn playing the bass guitar.   © Ron Howard/Getty

Marc performs on television programme *Music in the Round* on 8 December 1971.

Above: The Tanx sessions, in 1972, at the Chateau d'Hérouville recording studio in France.

Below: Marc Bolan at the controls: Rosenberg Studios in Copenhagen, 1972.

Above: Beatles drummer
Ringo Starr, dressed as
'Mouse', jokes around
with Marc during the
filming of *Born to Boogie*
in 1972.

Below: Marc, looking
resplendent in a leopard-
print blazer, is pictured
at the Palace Hotel in
Copenhagen. 1973.

Above left: Marc in concert at the Fairfield Hall in Croydon.

© *Ray Stevenson/Rex*

Above right: Marc in classic rock star regalia, power-posing with his iconic Gibson Les Paul guitar.

© *Michael Putland/Getty Images*

Below: T. Rex at the top of their game. Gloria Jones can be made out on the far right, singing backing vocals.

© *David Warner Ellis/Getty Images*

This 1973 concert in Essen was the last live show T. Rex played in Germany.

Left and below right: The ever-changing faces of Marc Bolan: in 1976 Marc embraced a new look, temporarily shorn of his lustrous locks.

(© Michael Putland / © Malcolm Goy)

Below left: From a television appearance on *Rock On With 45*. Taken 1975.

© Rex

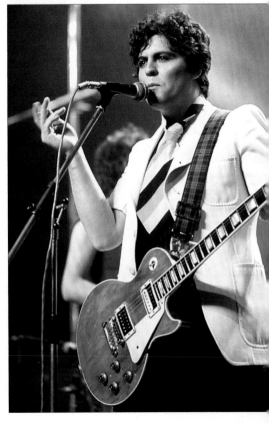

On 5 May, the T. Rex Wax Co. issued 'Metal Guru' and Fly released a greatest-hits package entitled *Bolan Boogie* on the very same day. Quite coincidentally, both single and album reached No. 1 in their respective charts, just two weeks later on 20 May. Fly could proudly boast their third No. 1 Bolan album in a row – a feat that the T. Rex Wax Co., unfortunately, would never match. The *Bolan Boogie* package contained thirteen tracks, of which four were the hits of 1971, plus, once again, a selection of Tyrannosaurus Rex titles.

Bolan commented to the press, 'I'm not at all happy about it and the remarks I made about the reissue of "Debora" apply equally to this album. Still, if the kids want to buy it, right on. It's flattering that people want to turn back the clock, as long as they realise it has nothing to do with what we are presenting now.'

'Metal Guru' was an easy choice for a follow-up single according to Marc himself, and an easy song to record in contrast to others: 'The band laid down their basic tracks in under two hours and went home, while Tony and I stayed on to get my guitar playing perfect. Which actually took a few more hours.' The engineers were then allowed to go home so that just Marc and Tony were left to give the sounds the feel they needed. Marc continued, 'The engineers are good guys, but we like to make the subtle changes in the sound that they might miss.' Marc then travelled to Los Angeles with the master tape of 'Metal Guru' to get his usual ex-Mothers of Invention to put down the backing vocals. Clearly, he was satisfied with the results, later stating, 'I think that "Metal Guru" is my finest single yet. The flipside tracks "Thunderwing" and "Lady" are pretty classy, too.'

Marc went on to explain a little more about the latter: 'The intro to "Lady" is Lennon and McCartney's "Eight Days a Week", intentionally. The rest of it is like a Sun [Records] oldie, a nice groove track, vaguely Spectorish with twelve acoustic guitars. It has the most instruments I've ever used, with Mellotron, and Howard and Mark's backup vocals.'

'If any of you fleshy thirty-year-olds snigger and snarl [about liking the single],' wrote unaccredited reviewer, 'I'll put me boots through your Chess sets, abuse your Tarot cards and eat your lousy Moody Blues albums . . . Bolan is ace cat . . . King Groover master of boat and swing-back boogie . . . [I]t's 1972, and there's an idol there for the idolising.'

Val Mabbs suggested, 'The catchy hook, string sounds come in and there is something of the feel of Spector about the way the whole is put together. Seems that an obvious effort has been made to get away from the familiar guitar riffs that have run through the more recent T. Rex singles, and the basis for this is the percussion chugging and powerful backing vocals.'

An uncredited reviewer, with obviously far too much time on their hands, enlightened us of the following completely unnecessary facts about this latest single: '"Metal Guru" occurs twenty-one times in the two minutes twenty-five seconds of the track. This results in a "Metal Guru" once every 6.9004762 seconds.' The reviewer, if you were still awake, went on enthusiastically, 'In the brief instrumental breaks you get a chance to observe exactly the near-Wagnerian battery of instruments and voices that storm and wail behind Marc's voice. There's a nice guitar line in there too, if you listen closely . . . Like him or not, Marc has worked out exactly what it is that makes a record work.'

On 6 May, Marc announced to the press that T. Rex were to go back on the road for a summer tour. This news was greeted with some surprise, as originally the Wembley gigs were to have been the last British dates that year until the autumn tour. 'The reaction at Wembley was such a gas,' the singer admitted. 'Many fans have complained that they could not get to London and so we are going to them, as we have done in the past.' The Birmingham Odeon on 9 June was to be followed by Cardiff Capitol (10th), Manchester Belle Vue (16th) and Newcastle City Hall (24th). It was also confirmed that there were to be two shows at each venue except for Manchester.

As if confirmation were needed that the tours were getting out of hand, the dates in June did just that. It was mayhem. Marc emerged from one gig with bruised ribs after a fight for his life when cornered by three female fans, all brandishing scissors and intent on taking a 'souvenir' from his head. The days of inviting one or two fans backstage to take a single lock of hair was no longer an option. It was never made official that T. Rex finished with touring in their home country, but the autumn tour promised just months earlier never materialised. The fans' behaviour may well have accounted for Marc's absence from the UK's shores. His personal safety was increasingly at risk.

An interview later in the year, with Jim Esposito in the USA, made the point clear: 'In England,' he confesses, 'I can't play any more, just for safety. When we did those Wembley concerts, we had nine big heavy cats and about five thousand chicks just wiped them right out. I had to be thrown in an armour-plated car and driven off. That was on national news . . . I dig it.'

Marc continues, telling Esposito, 'It's just people going absolutely crazy, trying to grab hold of you and stuff, but it's all right as long as you've got good security. It's exciting,' he says, without explaining what he means by 'good security'. He goes on: 'Everything's a hassle when you're touring. The only thing that isn't a hassle is when you're on stage. Everything else is an unbelievable strain. The only reason I do tours of any sort is purely for the pleasure of the people, to allow them to see what we're like live, and to experience the visual thing, I do it because I like playing, anyway.'

It could be argued that not gigging was the first mistake Marc made in judging the mood of his fans and it cost him dearly later in terms of his popularity. Excepting two Christmas shows, it would be two years before Marc toured England again, by which time much had changed.

Track Records had 'discovered' some old demos from Marc's pre-Tyrannosaurus Rex days under Simon Napier-Bell's management, and announced they were going to release them. The album was to be called *Hard on Love*. While admitting defeat with Fly and its constant stream of reissues, Marc ensured that Track – whose distributor was Polydor – did no such thing by taking out and winning a High Court writ on 27 June. Perseverance sometimes pays, though: when, in 1974, Track had another go at releasing the same material, now titled *The Beginning of Doves*, Marc seemingly gave up the fight.

Advance orders of 100,000 greeted the long-awaited release of *The Slider* on 23 July. Recorded earlier in the year, it was well received and during its first week reached No. 4 in the album charts. It appeared that a fourth No. 1 album within a twelve-month spell was on the cards. Sadly, it was not meant to be and *The Slider*, for all its slick sexuality, slowly dropped away over the coming weeks, prompting the question of whether the lack of 'personal' promotion had any bearing on its poor staying power. In my opinion, far more attention to the promotion of *The Slider* and the single 'Children of the Revolution' should have been made, as other bands were quickly establishing their own image with legions of teenagers. Whether Marc Bolan simply began to believe that he could leave England to conquer lands far away, or whether the decisions were taken out of his hands, we may never know.

Marc considered the album his finest to date. 'But I always say that, don't I?' he admitted, with a smile. *The Slider* was made to say what Marc really felt. He mused, 'I was going through a very low-key stage, and I should be respected for putting out what I wanted,' showing yet again his seemingly constant defence of his music. 'I was honest to myself when I put it down. But the new album is so electric – I don't even think there's one acoustic guitar on it' – there were actually acoustic-guitar tracks buried under all the electric, rhythm and strings – 'and, if there is, I can't hear it!' Becoming somewhat exasperated, Marc concluded that, 'I've watched them put me down for doing super commercial rock and roll, then for *The Slider*.'

So *The Slider* was important to Marc because it was the first album in which he had been lyrically true to himself. He even went as far as suggesting that the *T. Rex* and *Electric Warrior* albums were simply 'ideas'. *The Slider* – according to the singer himself – was the finished article. Many of the songs were self-portraits, some quite sad, and the beautiful

'Spaceball Ricochet' has always been acknowledged as an autobiographical title, much in the way that 'Teenage Dream' was viewed two years later. Many people have expressed surprise that 'Spaceball Ricochet' was never released as a single. On a personal level, I think it would have been an incredibly shrewd move and I would think that it would have sat nicely at the top of the charts. Marc, however, considered the number 'too laid-back' and not a 'suitable track for discos'.

In September 1972, Richard Williams of *The Times* wrote, 'Rod Stewart enjoys himself at the wheel of a yellow Lamborghini Miura. Marc Bolan can't drive, so he gets himself chauffeured around in a white Rolls. The papers haven't told me yet what mode of transport David Bowie prefers, but I'll bet it's something good. All three have been around for years, either ignored (Rod), laughed at (Marc), or nearly invisible (David). Bowie and Bolan are probably the most calculating rock performers Britain has spawned.

'When it comes to rock 'n' roll . . . *The Slider* is full of songs of a slightness which is wondrous to behold. But the hushed intimacy of Bolan's vocal delivery helps to make one word do the work of ten – particularly when combined with his gift of coining oddly appealing images.'

At the end of August, controversy broke after Marc's decision not to appear in France on a four-date tour. It was apparently cancelled because of reports from the French venues that ticket sales were disappointing. Not so, retorted the Bolan camp, insisting they had not had enough time to prepare for the forthcoming American tour. With that, T. Rex left on a flight to Montreal, Canada, for a single gig, which preceded the beginning of their second American adventure of the year, and it did not get off to a good start.

The band, or, more importantly, Marc Bolan, could not get the audience moving much at all. Initially, the atmosphere was none too friendly, either, with dissent from the front of the audience as first they heckled Bolan and then stood up – not out of excitement, but pure bloody-mindedness – to spoil the view of the fans seated behind them. At one point, the singer, who had been giving the set his all, stopped and shouted into the microphone, 'I feel that we're working damned hard up here, and not getting much response.'

Later, he said of the night, 'The gig was about twenty miles from the city. Plus, we had sound problems we don't usually have. I don't think we'll have to work that hard again on this tour.' And he added, 'At one point I thought I was going to die. I really did. But I don't mind lying on the floor. Whatever it takes.'

The day of the Montreal gig on 8 September, while Marc Bolan and T. Rex were touring their way to New York, 'Children of the Revolution' was released in Britain. 'I'm certainly not flattered that people want to use me. If I spend twenty-four hours in a studio I need nothing like being flattered and told what I've done isn't bad! But you can't fool the children of the revolution, that's it.'

The single entered the charts at a comparatively low No. 14 – the last T. Rex to have come in so low was 'Get It On' in 1971 – but the following week soared to No. 2, sitting behind Slade, who were enjoying their third week at No. 1 with 'Mama Weer All Crazee Now'. Expectations were high for a fifth T. Rex No. 1, but it did not happen.

Melody Maker's Chris Welch noted: 'With Mr Bowie the current "in" superstar and uncle Rod and Slade dominating the top singles chart positions, it will be interesting to see if T. Rex can continue their incredible trail of success.' To add to the list, David Cassidy blocked Marc, and then along came Lieutenant Pigeon with 'Mouldy Old Dough'. 'Children of the Revolution' never recovered; it spent the four weeks of October moving down the charts a few places at a time.

It was, however, to become the anthem for Bolan's followers, with a driving, throbbing beat that took a hold and unleashed all the emotions of growing up. It was chock full of brilliant lines ('I've got a Rolls-Royce 'cos it's good for my voice') and boasted the rallying chorus 'You won't fool the children of the revolution'. This was a classic song in what was largely a dreary, mixed-up chart. Marc declared that the song had been 'written for the kids who buy the records. I do my music for them and them only, and, if people in the media want to work with me and be my friend, they're super welcome.' There is, of course, a bittersweet irony here, as the anthem could have carried a warning to Marc himself: fooling his own fans could be a mistake.

As the single took its course in England, Marc was attempting to conquer America. Describing it later as an 'adventure tour', he had acquired the fuller choral sound he wanted at gigs by using Aretha Franklin's backing singers on most of the dates, as well as Joe Cocker's backing singers when in Los Angeles.

By his own admission, one of Bolan's problems in America was that T. Rex were not viewed there as a singles band. 'Get It On' – titled 'Bang a Gong' in the States because the original title was a sexual term in American-English slang – was the band's only Top Ten hit in the country, selling more than a million copies.

The other releases did nothing. 'It's only through lack of airplay,' Bolan maintained. 'Much like we had in the beginning in England. I'm convinced that things like "Magical Moon" and "Rumbling Spires" would have been hits if they'd been played.' More likely, Bolan's problem was that, while he considered himself the rock-'n'-roll Tolkien underground poet for American consumption, once on stage he was coming across as a sexual glider. In the States, this made him an unknown quantity and the lack of familiarity bred rejection.

In November 1972, T. Rex toured Australia and the Far East. Gradually, scenes reminiscent of the reaction the band had aroused back home – British reaction – began to bubble up, but somehow the experience did not have the same effect on Marc. *The Slider* was No. 1 in Japan when the tour began in Tokyo on 28 November. The promoters there had hired a complete clothes store for a T. Rex reception, where they also sold Bolan-style clothes – such hype was typical of the well-oiled promotional machine in Japan.

The year finished as it had started, with a new single. T. Rex released their fourth of the year when 'Solid Gold Easy Action' burst onto the scene. My first impression? 'How the fuck do you dance to this one at the youth club?' Personally, I loved it simply for its rawness and the crazy speed of the main riff; it had Marc Bolan and T. Rex written all over it. The single finished the year at No. 3 and would go one place higher in the first week of 1973. It was, incidentally, the first T. Rex single to have only one track on the flipside since 'By the Light of a Magical Moon', released in 1970, and this would remain the policy until 1975.

With 'Solid Gold Easy Action', Marc was feeling particularly confident, and, when I mentioned that, for me, his previous album *Slider* lacked the impact that *Electric Warrior* created, he commented, 'Well "Solid Gold Easy Action" will blow your radio apart.' In an interview just three years later, Marc divulged to Geoff Barton, '"Solid Gold Easy Action" sold 750,000 copies and I hated it. It sounds like the speed record of all time. It's too fast, but there you go, there you are.'

The new single was quickly followed by the announcement of the premiere of the motion picture *Born to Boogie* on 14 December. This was the documentary shot earlier in the year at the Empire Pool, Wembley, by Ringo Starr and his team. Its reception by the media was poor, but we fans loved it – which is only natural, considering that T. Rex had all but starved us of live action over recent months. Furthermore, this was the age before pop-promo videos, when even just two or three months of not seeing your idol could be soul-destroying for fans.

As 'Solid Gold Easy Action' was climbing the charts, Marc announced that he would be playing three special 'T. Rexmas' gigs, one at Edmonton Sundown on 22 December and the other as two houses at the Brixton Sundown on 23 December. The fans rushed to purchase tickets, priced at a keen £1.25, for shows that were quite simply stunning. All the regrets, all the bad feelings at having been deserted, melted away the moment Marc Bolan appeared on stage in gold-lamé dungarees. The sound was heavier, tighter than ever before, but the excitement had also changed. Yes, there was enthusiasm; yes, the kids were still screaming; but it was tempered by a little reserve, a desire almost not to annoy Marc and send him away again. The sound itself was more soulful – and what a showman! Bolan had entered a new era, but would it be enough?

Marc relished the filming of *Born to Boogie* and explained how it all began: 'Originally, Ringo came to me and said he was working on a project for a series of films that would probably make a TV series. He didn't go ahead with that project in any case, but the film itself got made.'

It was good timing because, earlier that year in March, when the idea was finalised, Bolan was about to enthral everyone at Wembley and Ringo Starr managed to film both performances. Additional filming was then carried out at John Lennon's country estate and at an airfield in Ripley. Finally, some studio footage, shot with Elton John, was added. Marc made the nature of the film very clear: 'It has absolutely no plot – it's just non-stop rock 'n' roll with studio and live sequences linked by comedy that's a little on the surreal side.'

The movie kicked off with its premiere on a Thursday evening at the Oscar One cinema in London's Brewer Street, Soho. The press kit, which came in a package of several parts handed out on the night, was put together by Marc and Ringo Starr's press agent. It is reproduced in part here:

PART ONE: BACKGROUNDER

Born to Boogie is, according to Marc Bolan who stars in it with T. Rex, 'a film with surrealistic overtones'. It is also a film laden with the music of the 'boogie hopper' complex; by that one means, 'it sells on disc' and will surely achieve a carbon 'Black' copy success for this Apple film which is produced, directed by and also stars Ringo Starr.

The film is about that which is happening in pop music – NOW! Among the fourteen songs (plus a reprise of many) are at least six Marc Bolan number one hits [*sic*]. It is not intended as a documentary of our time and moment, but simply an offering to appeal to those youngsters – maybe starting around eleven years and upwards – who just wish to hear their music, to be catered for, to be able to go to a cinema and see, hear, absorb and enjoy some 65 minutes prepared purely with them in mind. Certainly, if the records of Messrs Bolan, Starr, Elton John 'and other nuns' is any criteria, then they have the formula for success.

So – wherever you see *Born to Boogie*, please leave any preconceived ideas outside . . . and bring your teenage mentor into the warmth and rapport she or he will feel with this delightful film – made expressly with THEM in mind.

PART TWO: MARC BOLAN SUMMARISES THE RINGO STARR/ APPLE FILM BORNTO BOOGIE

The film was made purely as a piece of rock and roll entertainment. I feel it documents the phenomenon that has been T. Rex through the past year – and that was the purpose of the film initially. But as Ringo and I became more involved in the making of *Born to Boogie* we decided to add several more scenes, bringing in 'accidental' humour and to shoot 'live' without dubbing. By so doing we were endeavouring to get a spontaneity, which does not come naturally from some films.

In some of the scenes outside of the concert we let our imaginations take their course and, with the aid of props and a dwarf, let whichever happened, happen. And it did. We made the film strictly for a teenage audience who demand youthful excitement of the cinema as well as on television and in the theatre. I think the film does that – no more, no less.

In an interview for the USA publication *ZOO World* with Jim Esposito in 1972, Marc expanded on the subject of *Born to Boogie*: 'He [Ringo Starr] came along and wanted to do something. I've known Ringo for about five years, but not very well. [. . .] I didn't want any crap. I wanted some good things. I rewrote four or five surrealistic sketches and we booked an aerodrome. We got a couple of midgets, a small cannon, some fifty-foot statues – that kind of stuff. I dressed up like the Mad Hatter and Ringo dressed up like the dormouse. We just decided to see what we could get. We did some other things at Apple with Ringo and Elton John playing with us. [. . .] It was a gamble, and we were doing it literally for the kids. What we've gotten is probably the first rock 'n' roll film made by rock 'n' rollers. There's no big stars behind it. We did a picture with our own money.'

20th
CENTURY
BOY

T·REX
MARC 4

best selling singles group in England

1973

'I could retire tomorrow . . . but that's not what it's all about. If
I didn't work I'd freak out. I'd OD in two years and be found in a
gutter somewhere. I'm a rock-'n'-roller, I'm a guitar player, nothin'
else . . . I can tap dance a bit too though. And I bet you've never
seen me play the sitar with a toilet lid.'

MARC BOLAN

For all his stature as a pop musician in the early 1970s, it is a surprise that Bolan did not appear more often on television in Britain. He had a spellbinding effect on people with whom he came into contact. He could be aggressive as well as incredibly egotistic, but he could also melt hearts with the most innocent of gazes.

Until 1973, he had rarely been only seen on anything other than the BBC's *Top of the Pops*, which was the only television programme at the time to broadcast solely popular music. There were other shows that he graced, though. As we have seen, his debut on *Music in the Round* in the spring of 1972 (recorded some four months earlier on the 8 December 1971) had been well received. T. Rex appeared on Cilla Black's show *Cilla*, screened on the evening of Saturday, 27 January 1973.

They played a new track, 'Mad Donna', from the forthcoming

album *Tanx*, and Marc then sang an acoustic version of 'Life's a Gas' as a duet with Cilla. The duet was gushy, to put it mildly, but the appearance caused a storm of protest from the usual group of killjoys who felt that Marc's sexual gyrations (as they chose to describe his performance during 'Mad Donna') were inappropriate for a Saturday-evening show. This had strong echoes of the flak Elvis Presley attracted for his 'scandalous' appearances on US TV in the 1950s.

The fans did not object, though, as it gave them another all-too-rare glimpse of Bolan and the band. If British fans thought that Marc's slot on Cilla Black's show was the beginning of a period of high-profile appearances, however, they were sadly mistaken. T. Rex spent February 1973 in Germany and Austria; British fans were now having to learn to share him. What's more, other pop idols had begun to break through in 1972 and in 1973 they became a serious threat to his status: Gary Glitter, the Sweet and Slade were all to notch up more hit singles than Marc during this year.

Not until 2 March did T. Rex issue their first single of 1973. With advance sales exceeding 100,000, it was of little surprise that '20th Century Boy' entered the singles chart at a very respectable No. 3. The single was fast, furious, aggressive and heavy, the opening power chords sending out a clear message to the gathering band of Bolan knockers who claimed that Marc was finished and that all his songs sounded the same. 'This is my best single yet . . . or could be,' he declared with a mischievous smile, oozing confidence.

The old formula still haunts your senses, and after one or two plays everyone is hooked. '20th Century Boy' was kept at No. 3 yet again by Slade (at No. 1 with 'Cum on Feel the Noize') and the American heartthrob Donny Osmond (No. 2 with the slushy 'Twelfth of Never'). The week that the single reversed to No. 5, T. Rex released the new album *Tanx*. It went straight in at No. 4, just as *The Slider* had done the previous year. It then spent a second week at No. 4, but thereafter the album slowly reversed. *The Slider* had been a slick and sexually aggressive album of pop songs.

Tanx exhibited even more polish than Marc had claimed for its predecessor, and was both more direct and equally clever – allowing for the layers and layers of sounds that hit you square between the eyes. Bolan chose this album – consciously or not – in defiance of the media, who had suggested that Marc was a spent force. At such a tender age, I had no knowledge of the constant griping that appeared to fill so many column inches in the music press. Looking back through masses of written material, I am amazed that Marc was still able to produce anything. All I knew was what Marc put in front of his fans and, as far as we were concerned, he could do no wrong. *Tanx* yet again showed that Marc Bolan never stood still. Every new album and every new single was for me nothing more or nothing less than a journey through the mind of my music idol.

Marc enjoyed a small rumble of outrage with the cover and advertisement photographs for *Tanx*: he sat astride a tank, its gun barrel in an upward position, closely resembling an erection. Was it deliberate? Probably! One member of the public wrote in to a music-paper letters page and declared the sight to be 'provocative and pornographic': 'Not content with producing "Teenybopper Trash" for doting hordes of thirteen year olds, he now produces this picture which can only be described as an obscenity.' The letter is especially derisory as the writer states at the beginning: 'Having just been shown the advert for the latest T. Rex LP, *Tanx*, I feel I must voice my anger,' but then reveals his true colours when he admits: 'I have not heard the record myself.' Some things never change. A spokesman for Bolan countered with, 'I've never seen an obscene tank in my life, although armoured cars are slightly depraved.'

In April 1973, if you were among the 450 fans going to see ELO at the Watford Town Hall, you would have been surprised to see a very special guest join the band on stage for their encore – a pulsating rock medley ensued, getting a mighty big slice of glitter dust. Keith Altham, Bolan's publicist at the time, explained: 'Marc and Jeff Lynne, [ELO's] lead singer, are very old friends and have done a few sessions together. [Marc] often goes along to see the group.'

The band had known Marc for many years, including those early Tyrannosaurus Rex hippy days, when Jeff Lynn had been in a band known as the Idle Race. The spontaneous get-together had been sparked earlier in the day when both Marc and ELO were recording at the legendary AIR studios in London.

In 2012, Bev Bevan, ELO's drummer, was to recall the day for a local paper, the *Sunday Mercury*. 'We were at Air [Studios] London, putting down some new tracks for an album [*On The Third Day*] when who should walk in but Marc, who had been recording there earlier in the day . . . [W]e got down to work with Marc joining us and we completed a couple of tracks. Listen to the single version of "Ma Ma Ma Belle" and it's Marc playing twin guitar lead with Jeff Lynne . . . One night in Watford, he turned up with his guitar and jammed with us on "Roll Over Beethoven" . . . Our audience were quite "heavy" and with Marc's pop image he came in for a bit of stick from some . . . but he soon won them over and we all enjoyed ourselves.'

After its release on 1 June, the new single 'The Groover' spent just five weeks in the Top Twenty listings. It peaked at No. 4 on the second week of release. With hindsight, perhaps, Bolan would have been better advised at the time to have been seen as well as heard. It would have been worth the trouble of arranging a few live dates to promote the album. This may well have caused security problems, such as those experienced the previous year, but no one was going to find out, as T. Rex spent the remaining two weeks of June in Germany recording new material. Perhaps the singer was becoming scared that the media were right. Perhaps he would not need the security after all. Perhaps his star was fading!

While 'The Groover' enjoyed its brief life in the charts, Bolan and the band took off for Munich to start recording tracks for their next album. Two of the backing singers from the last American tour were invited to Munich to do some backing vocals, as Marc had been immensely impressed by one of them in particular, and had felt that her soulful voice would work well with his new ideas.

When Gloria Jones was contacted in America and invited to work on sessions again for Marc, she was delighted. She approached a friend, who had also appeared on the previous T. Rex tour, to join her at his request, only to discover that she was not available. Gloria turned to another close friend whom she had known since childhood: Pat Hall, a Southern gospel singer, who fortunately was free to work. The ensuing partnership of these two 'soul sisters' was to knock Marc sideways. The backing sounds they created were unique to T. Rex and musically worked incredibly well.

The band were also expanding in other ways. Prior to beginning a six-week tour of America in July, Marc Bolan signed up guitarist Jack Green. With Gloria Jones and Pat Hall also invited on the tour, Marc felt, with justified confidence, that the new and live T. Rex were ready for America – but was America ready for T. Rex? The tour was gruelling and Bolan's obsession with America was becoming all-consuming, to the extent that those around him feared the worst.

June Feld was to disclose to me that, in her opinion, this fixation was the first real crack in all Marc's relationships. They took in thirty-one dates, starting at Milwaukee on 20 July and moving from city to city, including Chicago, Memphis, Kansas, Davenport, Miami, New York and Los Angeles.

On this tour, they were the opening act for Three Dog Night and initially the fans' reactions to T. Rex were not encouraging. There was a polite response, but nothing dramatic; however, this did not remain the case. Slowly but surely, fans started appearing at the concerts wearing glitter makeup, and Marc Bolan began to get feedback from the crowds. In Memphis, the first signs of acceptance appeared when more than just a few fans got off their seats and danced to the beat. The band were tight and perhaps Marc's dream of conquering America would be possible after all.

After a brief holiday in the Bahamas during September, Bolan and T. Rex spent October first touring Japan – where they played to packed houses in cities including Tokyo, Nagoya and Hiroshima – and then moving swiftly on to Australia, where a four-date mini-tour started at the Hordern Pavilion in Sydney on 3 November. This was followed by appearances at the Apollo Stadium in Adelaide (6th), the Festival Hall in Melbourne (7th) and finishing at the Festival Hall in Brisbane (10th). Paradoxically, while Marc was doing well elsewhere in the world, the UK was slowly turning its back on him.

The T. Rex Wax Co. issued an album titled *T. Rex Great Hits*, which was mostly shunned by the fans and became the first T. Rex album not to enter the Top Thirty (it made No. 32). 'Truck On (Tyke)', the third single of the year, was released on 16 November to derision by the press. Marc had to rely once more on a hard core of fans to chart the single. The initial chart position of No. 20 was his lowest in over three years and, worse still, it was his first single not to enter the Top Ten since 'By the Light of a Magical Moon' in January 1970.

On the completion of the T. Rex tour of the Far East, a spokesman for T. Rex announced that Bill Legend had left the band. Bill's explanation was that he had been on the road with them for almost three years and his personal life had suffered greatly; quite simply, in his own words, 'the fun and magic had died'. It was a shock to the faithful and triggered fresh worries about the future. Those concerns were underpinned by the polls: T. Rex were voted only the sixth-best singles band of 1973 in the NME poll, finishing below Dawn (1), Slade (2), Wizzard (3), the Sweet (4) and the Osmonds (5). They featured in no other categories. Had Marc Bolan's crown slipped a little?

PART THREE

PAIN AND LOVE

Whatever happened to the... Teenage Dream?

Marc Bolan's first Solo Single; Out Now

RECOLLECTIONS

What of the planet thoth, what of lukenia
And the rusted blades of morgengast.

And tallow, brave tallow, will I ever
Again drink mead with that exalted warrior?
Ah such thoughts are perilous to my mind
In such a murky century as this,
And my casket of bones pleases me not.
For how could it when I have dwelt in one
Of the lithe bodies of thoth.

Wind. Yes, I liken walking in a thothen
body as to being akin to boreas the
windling.
And such tastes upon my Purple
Tongue hung, murch fruit, ripe and chosen
With care, tandon and chaladar of purnce
All a galaxy sweeter than Englands
brightest apple or an orange from the
meadows of Caloferina.
I wonder what vhirl is doing now,
I think of her Often, Often.

From the published 2015 collection of poetry,
Marc Bolan – Natural Born Poet

1974

'If God were to appear in my room, obviously, I would
be in awe, but I don't think I would be humble. I might cry,
but I think he would dig me like crazy.'

MARC BOLAN

In January 1974, Chris Welch arrived at the T. Rex office to
interview Marc. The building was in darkness – not caused,
as Welch explained in his piece, 'by an official day without
power but by a blown LEB fuse'. A picture that could have
been repeated in any household in the UK at the time – minus
the gold discs, of course. Britain had just entered what was
to be a seven-week national strike that affected electricity
supplies and caused other hardships.

Welch continued, 'Candle light glinted on the gold singles, a
huge rocking horse gave a Victorian touch, and the star himself
lightened the air of gloom by bursting in to dispense banter
and alcohol. [. . .] Seating himself on a black Chesterfield, his
hair seemed to have grown a bit longer than recent pictures
depicted, and he was tanned by a recent holiday in the sun.'

Marc briefly – and surprisingly – touched on politics, a

rarity for him, saying, 'I don't think anybody thought we'd ever get into the predicament we're in now, and I don't want to get too political, but suddenly it's inconvenienced everybody.' Soon enough, talk would move on to matters musical. Marc explains, 'I really wanted to use Elton [on 'Teenage Dream'], but he was out of town. I wrote the lyrics in the studio and lyrically it's pretty important. I thought of everything that day that had influenced me, and I very rarely do that. I had a melody and knocked out five verses . . . Originally there were nine verses, but I took some off because it got too obscene.'

Musically, the first two weeks of 1974 opened with the 'Truck On (Tyke)' single floating out of the Top Twenty. Bolan announced that T. Rex were to tour the United Kingdom, for the first time since 1972, opening at the Newcastle City Hall on 21 January, finishing at the Birmingham Odeon on the 28th. An announcement was also made about the new T. Rex line-up. Guitarist Jack Green had joined Mickey Finn and Steve Currie during the summer of 1973, but had not yet been seen by British fans. Nor had Gloria Jones and Pat Hall, and there was also the exciting addition of two drummers: Davey Lutton and Paul Fenton. The final surprise came in the shape of two saxophonists.

The fans were in for a treat, as the new line-up gave T. Rex a much heavier and fuller sound – the driving beat supplied by the two drummers was quite incredible. Davey Lutton's previous experience linked in well with former Carmen drummer Paul Fenton.

Marc reminded us all that there was no fooling the children of the revolution by treating us to a performance that erased the previous eighteen months without a live gig in the UK. Not everything was perfect – in fact, there were times when Marc seemed just a little rusty – but who cared? He was back with his own brand of panache – although now the sequins and satin were missing. Instead, now he had arrived on stage courtesy of a giant illuminated star that announced spectacularly that Marc Bolan was back in town, jeans and leather were now very much in evidence. Only Marc could reinvent himself in such spectacular fashion.

The Glasgow Apollo gig, the second on the tour, opened with the strangest support band imaginable: Chilly Willy, who played a set consisting of country music and old swing, and found themselves fighting, as others had before them, to be heard against the chants of 'Bolan, Bolan'. The Chilly Willy set complete, the audience awaited the first glimpse for far too long of Marc on stage. In massive flashing lights, the backdrop heralded the arrival of T. Rex. The glitter had all but gone. Bolan emerged on stage, to a tremendous welcome.

The band launched themselves into '20th Century Boy', to be greeted by a huge bellow of appreciation – a sound much like the collapse of a brick wall. 'The Groover', 'Jeepster', 'Telegram Sam', 'Metal Guru', 'Hot Love' and 'Get It On' were all pounded out to the loyal gathering. During a break between songs, Marc announced to his audience, 'Later this month, my new single, "Teenage Dream", will be released. I cut it in America some time back and, to be honest, I reckon it's one of the best singles I've done.'

The new single was greeted with caution. The fans had been trapped in a time warp, through no fault of their own.

Marc had seemingly deserted the very fan base he spoke so passionately about and they found this new, slower approach somewhat disconcerting. Personally, I was enthralled and loved every note, every line, of 'Teenage Dream', because this song epitomised my own journey through life. It was the first T. Rex single of the New Year, released on 26 January 1974, but appeared in the charts at a disappointingly low No. 18. It was to be T. Rex's only Top Twenty hit out of three attempts in 1974. One could not help but ask that very same question: what had happened to our own Teenage Dream – the once beautiful, elfin face of glam rock?

In the early nineties, while putting together a new TV documentary on Marc called *The Legendary Years*, I did an interview with Mickey Finn and I rather cheekily asked him to name his favourite T. Rex song. He had to think about it and at first was unable to come up with an answer. Then his face lit up. 'I tell you which record I did, like, which we haven't mentioned so far, was "Teenage Dream".'

I responded: 'It was very autobiographical on so many different levels.' Mickey agreed: 'Yeah, I think so and I think that, well, it's funny you should say that. He was – how can I say it? – he was in the right mould there with "Teenage Dream"; he just never developed it. I mean – I think that when that was picking up he should have moved into something . . . not self-analysing, but looking at things from a different angle! You know, I think that would have been a nice direction . . . for me, anyway.'

When the single was released, Marc himself commented: 'The point about the single is that I always say each one is different from the last, but everybody says they all sound the same. I won't comment on this one. But, if anybody says it sounds like *Get It On*, I'll blow 'em up!'

It was to be a while before the Bolan of old was to re-emerge – by which time it was almost too late. Musically, he had matured a great deal, as indeed had many of his fans. He had passed through his pop-star phase of 1972–3 and, while he had enjoyed that period, what was happening for him now was much more important. Marc himself was to say that he had got far too mixed up in the teenybopper adulation that also swamped David Cassidy and Donny Osmond. 'Any rock star can do that' was his response to those days.

Life itself meant much more to the new Marc Bolan; he had never been so free to be himself and get back to enjoying his music. 'Teenage Dream', as far as he was concerned, was lyrically the best single he had ever recorded: 'I'm proud of it. Unintentionally, it's very different.'

Different it certainly was: the song was mellow and outward-looking, while tinged with self-reflection. The strings were stunning – reportedly requiring a forty-piece orchestra – with a beautiful piano accompaniment played by Lonnie Jordan of the band War. All far removed from white swans, magical moons and metal gurus! Marc explained more during an interview with Chris Welch for *Melody Maker* in 1974: 'The idea of the song, is whatever happened to the enthusiasm one felt at the age of twelve, and why is one's first screw a drag, no matter how good the second one is?'

'Teenage Dream' had a very complicated lyric, much of which I have always believed was autobiographical, even though Marc himself dismissed this notion: 'The whole song doesn't necessarily apply to me, although some verses do.'

The reviews were polarised. One uncredited writer eulogised: 'Good old Marc! Just when everyone had given him up for dead, submerged under a pile of tuneless drivel, he comes up with a good single. It has good lyrics, an incredibly memorable refrain, and above all, it's different . . . Undoubtedly, some people are going to hate it, but that is nothing new to T. Rex. And this time Marc Bolan will have the last laugh.'

The new album was awaited eagerly. By Marc's own admission, T. Rex had evolved. What he now had was a solo career with a tight group of musicians and singers backing him, Marc Bolan and T. Rex now reborn as Zinc Alloy and the Hidden Riders of Tomorrow. This allowed Marc the scope to bring in changes, without confusing his fans. And he certainly wasn't going to countenance a rerun of the uncertainty surrounding the band's survival in 1969, when Tyrannosaurus Rex parted company with Steve Peregrin Took.

On the first day of February, *Zinc Alloy and the Hidden Riders of Tomorrow: A Creamed Cage in August* was issued. The album was credited to Marc Bolan and T. Rex, but this was not how Bolan had planned it. When the album artwork was first delivered to EMI, the names Marc Bolan and T. Rex were nowhere to be seen. The artwork was innovative for its time: a cream-coloured sleeve with an interwoven photograph of Marc in its centre; the album's title was written in a flowing, ink-pen style. The sleeve opened upwards and to either side each movement took a little of the image of Bolan with it, finally to reveal an airbrushed portrait of his face. In the bottom right-hand corner, in the same style as the name, was the subtitle: 'A Creamed Cage in August'.

The words 'Zinc Alloy' were meant to refer to Marc's alter ego. They came from a remark made a couple of years earlier, when he had jokingly told a reporter that once he was famous he would change his name to Zinc Alloy and wear an aluminium suit. EMI were horrified and advised Marc that this would be nothing short of PR suicide: it had become difficult enough as it was to sell T. Rex product to a sceptical public.

Marc relented on not only one but two changes. The first was that the names Marc Bolan and T. Rex would appear on the front of the sleeve, ending up as a red strip across the left-hand corner, and the second involved a limit to the run of luxurious sleeve packaging. As far as EMI was concerned, such lavish presentation was not appropriate with the then paper shortage (due to the Arab embargo on fuel supplies to the West). The popup sleeve therefore became a numbered limited edition, after which the design of the album would revert to a flat gatefold.

The album itself was slated by the press – and, overall, the fans seemed to agree with the media reaction, as sales were disappointing. This was unfortunate, because the album – now recognised as a joint production between Marc Bolan and Tony Visconti – contained some fine tracks. Many of them could be labelled 'progressive' and – in my opinion – were way ahead of their time. I have often wondered whether this leap forward was partly due to the singer's insistence on having much more production control.

The album today stands up well among the classic Bolan offerings, and it is a shame that, although Marc was now gaining more respect among fellow musicians, it was apparent that the public, the media and – most importantly – the hard-core fans remained unimpressed. The album peaked at No. 12, the lowest album chart position for the band in over four years.

At the beginning of March came a shock announcement: Tony Visconti was to depart. It was stated that he was leaving the T. Rex stable 'with regret' after nearly six years of musical association. The reasons for the split were acknowledged as 'musical differences', but I have always suspected that Marc simply felt he wanted to follow his own path. In *The Record Producers*, Visconti explained that the formula of the T. Rex sound really had not changed since 1971, when 'Get It On' was recorded: 'I could wake up in the middle of the night and set up a Marc Bolan sound for you on the desk, or a Marc Bolan mix, within five minutes.'

'The Children of Rarn Suite' was a Bolan project close to Tony Visconti's heart. It was meant to have been a concept albu n in its own right. The original idea was that of a musical version of something like Tolkien's *Lord of the Rings*, where a young man becomes the saviour of a mythical world called Rarn; it is narrative, representing the classic fight of good against evil. The opening and closing sequences of the 1970 *T. Rex* album hinted at its eventual release.

Visconti claimed that, each time Bolan went into the studios afterwards, he would ask the singer whether the new album would be *The Children of Rarn*, and Marc would agree and then promptly abandon the idea as soon as he started recording. Finally, Visconti lost patience when the promised 'Children of Rarn' concept was shoved aside for

Zinc Alloy . . . 'I just handed in my notice,' he explained. 'I never thought *The Children of Rarn* was going to materialise, and, in fact, it never did [during Marc's lifetime].' Tony Visconti counted himself one of Bolan's closest friends and the split upset him greatly.

Had Bolan lived, would he and Visconti have worked together again? Perhaps. But the singer managed to carry on without him. In an uncredited interview much later in the year, Marc said of the split, 'It kind of happened on its own. I wasn't happy with what was coming out of the relationship towards the end. It gets to the point where you have learned all there is to learn from someone. Tony is a folk producer really and he wasn't energising me any more. I can energise myself very easily . . . I'm a fucking good producer. It doesn't matter whose name is on the album cover, just as long as the sound is coming out right. It was ceasing to sound the way I wanted it to. I began to realise that it wasn't urgent enough.'

I asked Mickey Finn in my interview whether he felt hat Marc had discarded Visconti, or at least allowed him to leave, far too easily. '[I] don't really think it was a case of that. I think they simply grew apart,' he explained. 'You know, Marc did like to take control of everything and as the songwriter he had every right – but he found it very difficult to delegate.

'Tony and Marc used to disagree on things, but who doesn't? I do not believe that the split was a conscious thing and, in fact, I feel it had more to do with the real problem of Tony not always being available exactly when and where Marc needed him to be when recording . . . when we were touring, we would grab some recording time – in Japan, for instance. Visconti would not be there with us, and so Marc would produce instead. That is really how it happened.'

'So, it was purely accidental?' I suggested.

'Well, perhaps, accidentally on purpose!' Mickey responded, with a knowing smile.

On 13 July, 'Light of Love' was released and it was clear that only dying embers of support for Marc Bolan were now left: the single reached a low-profile No. 22. The band line-up had changed yet again by now, with the loss of Paul Fenton and Pat Hall and the arrival of Dino Dines, a keyboard player. Recorded in Los Angeles, the sound of the single was distinctly American-oriented, a solid beat with a sprinkling of funk. Sadly, it did not match up to the spirited change that Marc had so confidently pioneered during the *Zinc Alloy* sessions and the 'Teenage Dream' sound. Yet another change in direction, and one that proved costly.

Bolan left the UK for the shores of America once more in the summer of 1974. Gloria Jones, by this time publicly known as his partner both musically and personally, went with him. The split with June Feld had occurred at the tail end of 1973, with Gloria being cited as the other party in the subsequent divorce proceedings. Marc needed to be in the States because there were details of a projected tour to be finalised, as well as a new recording deal to be struck – his contract with American giants Warner Brothers, with whom Marc had been for some three years, was about to finish.

The 1974 tour of America started on 26 September at the Tower Theatre in Upper Darby, Pennsylvania. The next day saw T. Rex play Worcester, Massachusetts, before returning to Pennsylvania to play in Johnstown on the 28th. The bill was shared with Blue Öyster Cult.

Moving on to a club called Joint in the Woods, Parsippany, in New Jersey, on 2 October, T. Rex appeared in the late-evening spot to give the East Coast fans a taste of new material, including 'Solid Baby', 'Precious Star', 'Zip Gun Boogie' and 'Token of My Love'; at that time all were unreleased tracks. They also treated the audience to some oldies, including 'Jeepster', 'Get It On' ('Bang a Gong') and 'Telegram Sam'.

There followed a gap of some four weeks before the band were seen gigging again. Natalie McDonald – who published, along with several fellow American Bolan fans, a quite brilliant fanzine titled *Electric Warrior* – reported in Issue 3 that Marc had fallen ill and had had to cancel several dates in California and one in New York.

As he was about to get back on the road in the States, in the UK the T. Rex Wax Co. released 'Zip Gun Boogie' backed with 'Space Boss'. It spluttered to No. 41, and with it the humiliation was complete. Marc was later to blame 'mistiming' as one of the reasons for this, his first real flop since he'd become a rock star. He was getting even closer when he admitted that the lack of promotion was also responsible, but he attempted to shrug it off by listing the failures of other pop luminaries too: 'There's a lot of reasons. One of them was mistiming – I mean John Lennon's one flopped and Stevie Wonder's; it was mainly due to the combination of not being around for a year and a half – you can't put records out with no promotion – and the wrong time of year. Still, at least I flopped in good company.'

Back in America, on 9 November, T. Rex appeared at the

Roberts Stadium in Evansville, Indiana. The Guess Who – a band who had scored a No. 19 in England in 1970 with 'American Woman' – also appeared on the bill. Next stop was the Agora Ballroom in Cleveland, Ohio, on 11 November, where the gig was broadcast live on a local radio station, and the support band was Carmen, the band for whom Paul Fenton had drummed before joining T. Rex. Four days later, T. Rex appeared alongside the Sensational Alex Harvey Band at the Trenton War Memorial Theatre in Trenton, New Jersey, and the following day they were support to ZZ Top at the Capitol Theatre in Port Chester, New York. The tour ended at the Michigan Palace, Detroit on 22 November.

BOLAN'S

New Album on EMI

ZIP·GUN

BLNA 7752

Available on Cassette and Cartridge

EMI Records Limited

1975

'Artists go through hot and cold periods so I've just waited
for the time when I felt hot. Meanwhile I've written five
books, three screenplays, and ninety-five songs, and now I
can use all that material on the road.'

MARC BOLAN

The year 1975, in T. Rex years, was a comparatively quiet one, yet they continued to make music. *Bolan's Zip Gun* was released on 16 February, but Marc's concept of the album appeared to differ wildly from what the public expected. The tracks were, quite simply, too far removed from what the fans had hoped for and wanted. Many of them gave up and ignored the album, resulting in poor sales and little acclaim. There was nothing left of the Bolan of 1971–3, which was a bitter pill to swallow. Ironically, *Bolan's Zip Gun* is now regarded as another T. Rex classic. Aside from a couple of arguable exceptions, the album features many excellent tracks, notably 'Solid Baby', 'Precious Star', 'Think Zinc' and the quite stunning 'Till Dawn'. As with *Zinc Alloy*, all were way ahead of their time.

It is by far the most difficult T. Rex album to pinpoint and label. 'It's very simplistic. There's some pretty little songs on it and I play marimba on one of the tracks, which is a big kind of xylophone, plus all the guitars, keyboards, Mellotron and a few other things,' Bolan revealed at the time. 'My favourite tracks are "Solid Baby", "Girl in a Thunderbolt Suit", a few others. It's definitely the nearest thing I've done to *Electric Warrior*,' he enthused. 'It's very commercial, a kind of rock-'n'-roller, whereas the other one, which should be released two or three months after *Zip Gun*, has a much bigger kind of sound and I'll be arranging all the strings on it.'

When the announcement was made that Mickey Finn was to leave T. Rex, many felt that the band were finished for good. Unlike the loss of Bill Legend, and to a lesser extent Tony Visconti, Mickey's departure was seen as the break-up of the very heart of T. Rex – and with good reason. He had been a part of the set-up almost from the beginning and was nearly, though not quite, as synonymous with T. Rex as Marc himself. Finn's leaving has never been fully explained.

Mickey opened up to me while being interviewed in 1992: 'We were in Los Angeles and I was very indecisive; everybody else wanted me to go back home. First, Steve and Bill went home, then Marc and Gloria went home, and they all left me there. Well, they didn't leave me there. I had me choice and I thought I am going to spend some time and just hang out – you know, I wanted to go to a restaurant and go to a bar, I just didn't want anything to do with music. It was then I realised, and that was the last time I worked with Marc. We met a few times and everything and it was a very sad thing and we just split.'

I put to Mickey that there was an irony in the way it came to an end because it ended suddenly, just as it started suddenly some six years previously. I then suggested that perhaps, with hindsight, Mickey should have hung in there. Mickey pondered before admitting, 'To be honest with myself, which I must be first and foremost because it's important, I couldn't stay with the situation as it was. It's not because I didn't love him and loved the scene and obviously the money. I knew what I was doing but I did need a change. Maybe I was burnt out, maybe there was something wrong with me, but whatever it was it felt right.'

For his part, Bolan was in no mood to linger in the past and announced that a new T. Rex line-up would be arriving in England during July to do a few selected gigs. Shortly afterwards, on 21 June, came the release of the first T. Rex single of the year – 'New York City' – which, quite unexpectedly, put the band back in the Top Twenty. Revelling in this injection of new life, Marc suggested, 'For singles, I do try to pick out things that are perhaps easier to understand, less intricate than most. "New York City" was unlacing just that one image of a woman with a frog in her hand. I think that's amazing, don't you?'

Reflecting on the success, he argued that, 'Everybody said that after "Zip Gun Boogie" it would be really hard for me to get a hit single, but I proved them wrong. "New York City" was a hit single!'

There it remained for eight weeks, peaking at No. 15. Bolan had not lost all his mojo after all. The new T. Rex line-up comprised Steve Currie (bass), Davey Lutton (drums), Gloria Jones (clavinet and backing vocals), Dino Dines (keyboards) and Tyrone Scott (keyboards and backing vocals), and a mini-tour was arranged as a warm-up for the next full-scale British tour to be announced in the autumn. The band were billed as T. Rex, the 'Marc Bolan &' having been subtly dropped, and the ballroom dates were held at the Palace Lido on the Isle of Man on 13 July, followed by Tiffany's in Great Yarmouth on the 23rd, the Pier Pavilion in Hastings on the 25th and finally the Leas Cliff Hall in Folkestone on the 26th.

Why were the band playing such small venues? Marc's response was, 'We just want to play non-prestige dates, and renew our acquaintance with record buyers. We don't want to get involved in larger concerts.' This was greeted with some smugness by the media. He was later to confess, in an interview with Chris Welch for *Melody Maker*, that, 'I did those four crazy ballroom gigs a couple of months ago, with no promotion, just to see how things were. Would they just sit there and look at me? I didn't know. And they sold out, and the response was amazing, with no publicity. The local kids just turned out. And it went down well. But it could have bombed and, if so, we wanted to bomb in secret.'

On 26 September 1975, Marc Bolan became a father. Rolan was to be Marc's only child, a son by his girlfriend Gloria Jones. The singer held a press call and announced proudly that he had been there at the birth. Coincidentally, on the very day that Rolan was born, Marc released his second and last single of 1975. 'Dreamy Lady', credited to the T. Rex Disco Party.

One review was surprisingly kind: 'Strange beat from Monsieur Bolan on this follow-up to "New York City" – up-tempo and almost a soul rhythm . . . more acceptable than his previous record and as that was a big hit, this will probably do better.' The single enjoyed only limited success, however, reaching No. 30 in the charts.

Futuristic Dragon

OUT NOW

BLN 5004

T. REX ON TOUR

FEBRUARY 5th
CENTRAL HALL **CHATHAM**
FEBRUARY 6th
CITY HALL **ST. ALBANS**
FEBRUARY 7th
LEAS CLIFF HALL **FOLKSTONE**
FEBRUARY 8th
CLIFFS PAVILION **SOUTHEND-ON-SEA**
FEBRUARY 12th
FLORAL HALL **SOUTHPORT**
FEBRUARY 13th
PALACE THEATRE **NEWARK**
FEBRUARY 14th
GRAND PAVILION **WITHERNSEA**
FEBRUARY 15th
EMPIRE THEATRE **SUNDERLAND**
FEBRUARY 18th
LYCEUM **LONDON**

FEBRUARY 19th
QUEENSWAY **DUNSTABLE**
FEBRUARY 20th
WINTER GARDENS **BOURNEMOUTH**
FEBRUARY 23rd
TOWN HALL **BIRMINGHAM**
FEBRUARY 24th
FREE TRADE HALL **MANCHESTER**
FEBRUARY 28th
WINTER GARDENS **NEW BRIGHTON**
MARCH 1st
APOLLO THEATRE **GLASGOW**
MARCH 3rd
LARGE MUNICIPAL HALL **FALKIRK**
MARCH 4th
CIVIC CENTRE **MOTHERWELL**
MARCH 6th
GRAND HALL **KILMARNOCK**

With guest Lennie MacDonald

1976

'I've been back about three times, that I know of. I mean I get
these flashes and things. I was a minstrel and that would most
probably explain why I'm interested in literature, poems and
music and . . . I can remember being a cavalier as well.'

MARC BOLAN

Marc Bolan began the New Year by announcing the biggest
T. Rex tour in England since the *Electric Warrior*
concerts in autumn 1971. Between 5 February and 6 March
1976, they would appear at no fewer than eighteen venues. The
first major gig in the United Kingdom for two years kicked off
at the Central Hall in Chatham, Kent, taking in sixteen further
venues before finishing on 20 March at Motherwell Concert
Hall in Scotland. This was followed by a further series of
gigs: on the 23rd at Birmingham Town Hall, the Manchester
Free Trade Hall on the 24th and the Winter Gardens at New
Brighton on the last day of February. Scotland got its turn in
the first week of March with three dates: the Glasgow Apollo
greeted T. Rex on the 1st, Falkirk on the 3rd and Motherwell
on the 4th.

The tour went under the banner of 'Futuristic Dragon',

which was the title of the brand-new album to be released on 31 January. Marc revealed to Geoff Barton of *Sounds*: '*Futuristic Dragon*, my new album, isn't simple at all. You'll find that the lyrics of at least four of the tracks are very complex. Especially one called "Casual Agent" which is, well, I can't really give references, but it's like the equivalent of the "Scenescof Dynasty" from the early days.'

There were early signs of a reversal in the chart fortunes of T. Rex when *Futuristic Dragon* was listed in the Top Fifty, albeit only at No. 50 itself. Any initial optimism was dashed, however, when the album disappeared out of the charts and sank without trace. By this time, the tour was under way. There was a groundswell of support once more, but it was not sufficient to improve the chart position of the album.

The two major highlights of the tour were Manchester and Glasgow, areas where Marc's support had always been strong. On 21 February 1976, midway through the tour, another new single was released: 'London Boys'. Given the revived high profile of the band, and the quality of the single itself, it should have done better than its poor final position of No. 40.

The eighteenth T. Rex single, 'I Love to Boogie', was released at the beginning of June. It took four weeks before the track appeared – seemingly out of nowhere – at No. 17 in the singles chart. *Sounds* declared 'I Love to Boogie' as its star single of the week. Praise indeed: 'From the new Valentino Bolan . . . The time is ripe, I reckon for a Bolan revival . . . and could well be the resounding summer hit of 1976.'

The week after its initial appearance in the Top Twenty, 'I Love to Boogie' slipped down a place, only to recover the week after peaking at No. 13, to give Marc his biggest single in over two years. It was also, sadly, his last appearance in the charts before his death.

By the time the final T. Rex single of 1976 was released, on 17 September, Bolan had changed the line-up of the band for the eighth time since its inception and the fifth time since the end of 1973. Guitarist Miller Anderson became the latest recruit and, with his input, Bolan produced 'Laser Love', a slick but uncharacteristically heavy number that continues to confuse fans to this day.

Equally disorienting was his performance on *Top of the Pops* (in the days when established artists got to air their new singles before they charted), when he appeared with a brand-new image. He was dressed in a suit and tie, but the real shock was the hairstyle: the curls had been cut off and the hair slicked back. 'Bolantino' made his TV debut.

Record Mirror noted approvingly of the single: 'Stones riff marks this ultimate punky pop song from Marc. It's got two hooks, unbelievable lyrics, and the chance of being his biggest [hit] in years.' It was a new look alongside a new single but the same old resistance from the general public meant that, yet again, Marc failed to reach even the Top 40, albeit by a single position.

Later in the year, T. Rex took part in a live television special, *The Rollin' Bolan Show*, to be screened on Christmas Day, with heavy-metal band AC/DC as special guests. So it was that in December 1976, a very healthy Bolan – possibly looking his best since 1973 – graced the nation's TV screens. He had a renewed confidence about him that boded well not only for his own future, but also for fans, who had presumed that their idol's days were over.

One sad note was struck at the end of the year with Steve Currie's decision to leave T. Rex. Contrary to popular belief, Steve had been the band's longest-serving member – not, as many believed, Mickey Finn. Davey Lutton also moved on, but not through his own initiative, as Bolan wanted to change the feel of T. Rex and Lutton simply did not fit into his plans. Strangely, though, it left Marc Bolan in a situation not experienced in nearly a decade – a head full of dreams but no one around him musically to transfer those dreams into a finished product.

THEATRE ROYAL DRURY LANE

Proprietors: A.T.P. (London) Ltd.
Managing Director: Toby Rowland
Chairman: Lord Grade
Deputy Chairman: Louis Benjamin
General Manager: George Hoare

★★★★★★★★★★★

Christmas Supersonic

★★★★★★★★★★

In the presence of

Her Royal Highness, The Princess Margaret
Countess of Snowdon
President of The Invalid Children's Aid Association

in aid of

The Invalid Children's Aid Association
and
Stars Organisation for Spastics

with (in alphabetical order)
MARC BOLAN
THE G BAND
GARY GLITTER
GUYS 'N DOLLS
TINA CHARLES
JOHN MILES
TWIGGY
Musical Director:
HARRY RABINOWITZ

and guest artists
MARTI CAINE
CLIFFORD DAVIS
NOEL EDMONDS
ALAN FREEMAN
RUSSELL HARTY
JOANNA LUMLEY
NYREE DAWN PORTER

PRESENTED BY
THE DAILY MIRROR POP CLUB
SUNDAY, 19 DECEMBER, 1976

1977

'It's like if you take acid. It burns out brain cells and they
don't regrow. Rock is like that – it has killed beautiful people
musically, physically and mentally.'

MARC BOLAN

'What happened to *Laser Love?*' David Hancock asked Marc for *National RockStar* in January 1977. Marc responded, 'I'll tell you, "Laser Love" was a hit song but it wasn't a hit performance, which is why I broke up that T. Rex. The new T. Rex contains session ace Herbie Flowers and features Tony Newman, Miller Anderson and good old Dino Dines. We went in at nine o'clock in the morning to CBS studios, cut a "Laser Love" backing track in fifteen minutes, and it's fourteen times better than the record. And the record took me twelve hours.'

We can take it Mr Bolan was pleased with the band. Marc had seemingly got his groove back. Perhaps, as with everyone in life, there comes a time when you just know you have to look forward, not back. Marc realised that he could go into the studios, be confident, be excited, I would even suggest be re-energised. 'I booked AIR Studios that day and we cut four tracks. The new band is everything I've ever wanted.'

The release of a duet with Gloria Jones, 'To Know You Is To Love You', at the beginning of January 1977 left many confused and stunned. It was the first non-Bolan-penned A-side release. The song, having been written by Phil Spector, reached No. 2 in December 1958, courtesy of the band Teddy Bears. Perhaps this was Marc revealing to the world his love for his partner Gloria Jones. Regardless, the single failed to chart.

Alongside the news of the exciting new T. Rex line-up, a new album was announced, *Dandy in the Underworld*, to be released in February. With its arrival a breath of fresh air was blown into the whole vibe of T. Rex. Gone was the ego; the overindulgent production was kicked into touch. 'As far as Marc was concerned, the last two albums were a little thrown together and he was clearly not that pleased as an artist with what was finally released. Too much of Marc's time seemed to be spent sorting out contracts, not to mention his American deals that still needed to be resolved.' Bolan admitted to *Sounds* journalist Paul Morley, 'The last album was purely a contractual thing; plus, I wasn't happy with the band.'

Energy seemed to abound, with Marc revealing that *Dandy in the Underworld* was his most polished to date, and praising his new band. 'I wrote six tracks in the studio, and the rest had been around some time. It's a kind of cross between images and hard rock in a way that I've always wanted.'

It had stunning grassroots sounds; it cast me back to the way I felt about *Electric Warrior*. The album oozed class and mixed up rock 'n' roll at its finest with a sprinkling of Marc Bolan magic. Despite all the good vibes evidenced on the

Dandy tour, remarkably the album spent a short life in the Top 30 bestselling albums chart, spending just three weeks and peaking in the first week of April at a disappointing, if respectable, No. 26.

In the final months of Marc's all-too-short life Geoff Barton of *Sounds* summed up the man's magic succinctly: 'Bolan's talents may not have developed and matured over the years, but they have not diminished either. His tunes still inspire the listener to go right out and do that "Woodland Bop"; his voice still has that endearing quavering vibrato; his phrasing's still unusual, unique; his lyrics, nonsensically cosmic, still come alive; the image of the mischievous elf of *Unicorn* days still persists, even in the harsh light of the late Seventies.'

Marc Bolan had returned to basics – good old cosmic rock – and the sounds, while not so highly polished, were reminiscent of his *Electric Warrior* glory days. *Dandy in the Underworld* sold well, although never in sufficient numbers to get into the higher reaches of the UK album charts.

When the news broke that T. Rex were to go out and play major venues in the UK, I for one could not wait. My only frustration was that the band chose to play in France first. There was no Eurostar in 1977 and, to be quite honest, any travel outside of the UK was a challenge for me back then. So I had to swallow the pill of disappointment and wait for the UK dates to be formally announced. Bolan, however, had lost none of the tongue-in-cheek wit. Speaking to David Hancock for *National RockStar* in January 1977, he said, 'I decided to tour now because basically most of the bands around now are rubbish and it shouldn't be hard to prove my metallic metal, as they say.'

The last ten years had seen Marc change from folk singer to friend of the earth, from wizard to king of glam rock. He then morphed into a zinc-alloy demigod. So he arrived in 1977 as the father of punk. 'Not bad for a London boy that many wanted and waited to see fall from grace. However, survive he did, as only a true rock artist could. 'There probably are potential stars out there now, but they're just not reaching the people,' he says to Hancock. 'I won't say that my kind of star is a dying breed but you can't expect a meteor such as myself every ten years. I mean, you're talking about quality goods, you know.

'It doesn't worry me that I'm not selling as many records as I did in '72 because nobody is, including David [Bowie].' Marc tells Hancock earnestly, 'But the new album, which is coming out on 1 March, called *Dandy in the Underworld* . . . I can guarantee will be a Top Five album. It'll sell more than *Low*, anyway.'

The French tour actually kicked off on 3 February. Michael Green, on his excellent website dedicated to the 1977 Dandy tour (which I have drawn on for the gigography in Appendix A) notes that the tour has frequently been referred to as the 'warm-up' for the UK jaunt that was to follow. He points out, however: 'With seven concerts performed in France, this tour had only two less dates than the planned UK tour for the following month.' Green continues:

> The set list appears to be an abridged version of the one used in the UK the following month which had thirteen songs. At the Nantes gig on 3 February, T. Rex performed eleven songs, leaving out 'Debora' and 'Teen

Riot Structure' from the set – possibly because these two songs were still at the rehearsal stage or because of a time restraint imposed by the venue. Interestingly at T. Rex's appearance at Le Nashville in Paris on 11 February they also left out 'Telegram Sam' and 'Dandy in the Underworld'.

Michael Green also reveals five pages taken from Marc's own personal diaries of the French tour. I am indebted to Michael for allowing their inclusion here and I would suggest that anyone interested in seeing the original handwritten diary pages should visit his site [http://www.samgreen.co.uk/dandytour-france.htm] and see them for themselves. They are fascinating. Michael transcribed them to allow easy reading because, as is well known, Marc Bolan's handwriting could be wonderfully frustrating to read!

DAY ONE

Got up at eleven, o thou lazy rock star, felt good as today is the last day of rehearsal for the French tour, a kind of out of state dress run for the British tour to follow in March. While I dress, I play Bowie's new album, he's such a scallywag and also sly. He's [got] a great band, only like one song though in the car on way to rehearsal hall on Southbank [*sic*]. I read Richard Williams' piece on New York's rock intelligentsia – Television – great name. SOS, Mink DeVille, Tom Verlaine, sounds like an interesting brain to bend notes with.

We rehearse from 2.30 to 6. I'm really proud of this

band, Herbie Flowers bass, Tony Newman drums, Dino Dines keyboards, Miller Anderson 2nd guitar, vocals. We run through about 8 new songs from the forthcoming album, 'Visions of Domino', 'You Damaged the Soul of my Suit'. Some old biggies like 'Telegram Sam', 'Hot Love' and 'Get It On'.

DAY TWO

Today Gloria and I do Supersonic. I enjoy working with Mr Maestro [Mike] Mansfield. It's so unpredictable, today Mike has me 25ft up in the air on a swing, heavy insured I believe, and with Jones we sing 'To Know You Is To Love You' in a plastic bubble, filled with what feels like washing up liquid, waist high we croon, my toes and other things feel quite numb – a hard long day but never the less fun.

The tour awaits.

DAY THREE

Up to 6am [sic], I'd packed last night. The car comes at 7, it's still dark. Through force of habit I don a pair of shades and cat nap to we beach [sic] at Heathrow. Gay – o dear – Paris at 9.30 straight to the TV average telly day. Screened live at 6, I mime to 'Telegram' and our recent French hit, 'I Love To Boogie.'

It really motivates. I say bon voyage to the guys as I leave a day earlier to do a TV show and say I'll see them in France. Get home at 7, slip into something chic, pick and my partner [sic] in most things. Vocalist, producer, writer supreme Ms. Gloria Jones and make my way to have dinner with one Steve Harley, poet, singer and this night food financier. Had dinner at Julie's, a nice bistro accompanying Steve was his lady Yvonne. Altogether a magic restful evening, just what one needs before you start a tour, back at Steve's place I played him the title track from the new album, it's called 'Dandy in the Underworld'. Steve sings back-ups on it, he loved it, the only sad note was Cockney Rebel play a charity gig at the Rainbow on February 12 and Steve has asked me to do a number or two but unfortunately, we're in Paris. Shame it would have been sweet, home to bed.

DAY THREE

Up at 6am, I'd forgotten what leaving was like it's all coming back to me now. I fall out of bed, take a cold shower to the strains of 'New Rose' by The Damned, having packed.

Miming, strange but OK. I do some Elvis wiggles and talk to the viewers in a Charles Boyer accent.

DAY FOUR

The first gig. We're all excited. The place, a large club, is what is known as a warm up date, a gig to get sound, cues, lights and heads all in the right space for the big ones. The show feels tight. We blow for an hour and 10 and it's magic. All 10 days of intense rehearsal have payed [*sic*] off and I'm 100% pleased, it's been 2 years since I'd worked full throttle and it feels great to be expressing myself in the way I was born to do. After gig, we have dinner and see Johnny Hallyday – France's Elvis at a club. O La-La.

DAY FIVE AND DAY SIX

Driving through beautiful Basque countryside every view is like a French impressionist's heaven. I wish I could paint as well as pick. I just read *Myron* by Gore Vidal, great book it reminded me of Dylan's Tarantula – same chaos by [*sic*] more organised.

Finish[ed] lyrics to several songs that seemed unfinished in the chaos of the city, but become clear complete sonnets on the motorways of France. Next stop Paris.

Paris day – in morning went to the Louvre to look up a statue I'd enjoyed when I was in Paris at the cute age of 15. Hercules looked as great as I remember'd, also checked out Rodin's house, a museum with much of his work on view, just the artistic inspiration to key the Bolan brain for boogie.

When Marc announced the decision to take an up-and-coming punk band on the tour as support, was it a shrewd move or a massive mistake? The inclusion of the Damned had the potential to guarantee a new following. Marc allowed a little of his playful ego to creep in when he described himself, rather tongue-in-cheek, as the father of punk. Some members of the music media were sceptical. As a Bolan fan of long standing, I was far from enamoured of the idea of this polarised music fusion, but, at the same time, he had used worse support bands in previous years. I must admit, though, that I think my real issue was not being happy to share any live gig time with anyone other than Marc Bolan and T. Rex.

For everyone who attended the gig at the Rainbow Theatre in London's Finsbury Park on 18 March 1977, it was a night to savour. I felt hugely privileged to have been lucky enough to have seen so many Marc Bolan gigs over the previous decade, and being at Finsbury Park that night ranked alongside the Empire Pool triumphs five years to the day before – a fact I appreciated only many years later. It was also quite surreal to see such a mixture of Bolan fans with some very strange-looking 'kids' – well, they looked 'strange' and like 'kids' to my friends and me, anyway.

I was not that interested in seeing the support act the Damned, but got dragged in by my not-to-be-trusted Bolanite friends, who were curious about them. That curiosity introduced us to a rather volatile and slightly apprehensive meeting between two quite opposite genres of music. However, the shock to my system (emotionally and physically) ended with a great sigh of relief when the Damned went off stage.

At about 9 p.m., the main man appeared on stage, looking just dandy (no pun intended). Energy, panache and self-belief infused the atmosphere within the Rainbow, transmitted by the reborn Bolan I saw before me. Gone were the satins, silks and glitter. The flamboyant clothes of yesteryear had been replaced by a streamlined look of purple-mauve slacks and a stunning yellow jacket. The moment the band kicked in with 'Jeepster', I was lost in a re-landscaped Bolan heaven. It was not just the fact that it was one of the classic songs from a bygone era: it was the fact that this band kicked ass! The rest of the set showcased an equal measure of classics and tracks from the new album: 'Visions of Domino', 'New York City', 'The Soul of My Suit', 'Groove a Little', 'Telegram Sam', 'Hang-Ups', 'Debora', 'I Love to Boogie', 'Teen Riot Structure', 'Dandy in the Underworld', 'Hot Love' and 'Get It On'.

Between songs, Marc issued little soundbites, savouring his newfound connection; he grew in confidence as each song was met with enthusiasm and adulation. The tour had started on 10 March at the City Hall in Newcastle, followed by Manchester Apollo on the 11th, Glasgow Apollo on the 12th, Victoria Hall in Hanley on the 13th, Colston Hall, Bristol, on the 14th, Birmingham Odeon on the 17th, the Rainbow in London on the 18th, the Pavilion, West Runton, on the 19th and ending at the Locarno in Portsmouth on the 20th. It was the last tour Marc Bolan and T. Rex were to perform in the UK.

Not much has been made of Marc's decision to do a one-off gig in the Swedish capital of Stockholm after the Dandy tour had officially ended. The concert, on 24 May 1977, was at Gröna Lund – usually, the attraction there is the fairground, but it also boasts an outdoor stage. It seemed a strange place to finish off a tour. It is with a sense of irony that this concert was to be the very last that Marc Bolan ever performed.

At the time, Ulf Gustavsson was a reporter for, in his own words, a 'small provincial newspaper'. His report of the gig is reproduced here in edited form. My thanks to George Rab for allowing me to reproduce the following, which is copyright of the George Rab Archives:

> Bolan arrived on stage wearing this short yellow jacket and mauve trousers . . . they hit off with 'Jeepster', which was heavy and groovy, even though the sound quality was not the best. Bolan played his all-time greats mixed with practically all the songs from his latest album *Dandy in the Underworld*. The sound differed from earlier editions of T. Rex through Herbie Flowers' sharp, distinctive bass guitar, but also through Dino Dines' prominent part in the overall sound. It was a well-co-ordinated and terse band. Even though Marc Bolan's recordings from that year sound sterile, there was an evident pleasure playing live . . . I was impressed with [Marc's] guitar playing. He did long generous solos.'

Ulf clearly enjoyed the gig – although he and the crowd regretted that Marc had not heard them shouting for 'Children of the Revolution' – and afterwards he got the opportunity to ask the singer a couple of questions backstage. 'Marc was great in his generosity,' Ulf remembered. 'He was very sincere.' Asked about the band, Marc responded with, 'We have only been touring for about four months and the new band is fantastic. The excitement and the feeling are back now.' He continued, 'We work very well on stage. When we played at the Rainbow in London we met a very enthusiastic audience.'

Ulf asked Marc to pinpoint the difference between the old incarnation of T. Rex and the latest version. 'We are quite simply better now,' Marc replied. '*Electric Warrior* and what happened then was a good time, but it was six years ago. It got too much for a while . . . [I]n 1973 we toured almost continuously for seven months. I got bored . . . [Now] the old feeling is back. But we also have the technique now. The fingers play what the heart feels.' He added, 'Playing in Sweden was cold, but still fun. We only have a few old songs in the concert, the rest is all new material.'

And how did Marc feel about the *Zinc Alloy* album, a favourite of Ulf's? '*Zinc Alloy* was the last album with the old T. Rex, with very schizophrenic music,' Marc replied. 'The new album, *Dandy in the Underworld*, is a kind of confession.'

Marc had always dreamed of being a musician respected by his peers. He demanded that as his right – and believed he had earned it after ten years. He had paid his dues. He had matured, as had his songs. The album *Dandy in the Underworld* and the tour of the same name had heralded a mixture of slick *Bolan Boogie*, rock 'n' roll with a pinch of punk panache and euphoric self-confidence. The band awesome, Marc rejuvenated and with another new album on the horizon everything was falling once more into place.

Returning to England to enjoy the summer of 1977, Marc Bolan continued looking forward to a future buoyed by what appeared to be a mixture of old and new fans appearing at his gigs. This newfound optimism and positivity sadly did not rub off on the single 'The Soul of My Suit', a track lifted from the *Dandy* album, which failed to chart March.

Unfazed, Marc continued to believe enough in himself to

release what was to be his penultimate single in his lifetime: the title track from the album *Dandy in the Underworld*, but with a different edit for radio play (the reference to cocaine on the album track being removed). Once more, the live support did not carry over to single sales, hence it failed to chart after its release in May.

Sadly, the same fate befell the final single, 'Celebrate Summer', even on the back of weekly exposure, when Marc had his own teatime show simply titled *Marc*. The series, recorded during the last months of Marc's life, was aired late in August 1977 and tragically, by the time the last episode aired, Marc had died as a result of being a passenger in a Mini that left the road and crashed into a tree in Barnes during the early hours of the morning of Friday, 16 September 1977.

'We haven't much time to say what we want to say,' Marc told Steve Turner in 1972. 'The walls of eternity are closing in on us. I mean, whatever has to be done has to be done within the next ten years. But now I know that it's right – I've got to give everything now, while I can. Hendrix wasted the last two years of his life; just think what he could have done in that time. There is no time, I may not be here in two years, I don't know.'

The above quote is chilling, and, actually, it was not the first time Marc had had a premonition that, for him, time was of the essence. Perhaps it explains a great deal of the way he mapped out his life and the way, even from a very early age, he was driven by something deep inside his head. The most memorable incident, and one that will stay with me for ever, was when Shan and I found buried in the ITV vaults the now much-seen interview with Russell Harty from 1972. When asked about what he would be doing in twenty or thirty years, Marc went very quiet. The look on his face was haunting as he shook his head from side to side, indicating that he didn't think he would live that long, before quickly changing the subject.

One thing no one can be prepared for is life coming to an end. Over the decade I followed Marc Bolan, I would say without hesitation that he lit up my life – as he did for all his fans. Even now, four decades after his demise, he still fills all our lives with his music. We are fortunate that his legacy lives on and for that we should always be grateful.

Indeed, the purpose of this book was always to be a happy, positive fan's reflection on Marc Bolan, the beautiful dreamer. In the spirit of his life, the best way to remember Marc is in happier terms and, therefore, let us leave the last word to Mickey Finn:

I asked him, 'If you could take a single incident or a single memory of Marc, freeze it, put it in a bottle, what would it be?'

Mickey Finn: 'And if I do that, I could play it back repeatedly?'

JB: 'Repeatedly. As many times as you want to.'

MF: 'Well . . . we were in America and Marc had ordered all these clothes to come over in a trunk. [. . .] Anyway, the said trunk arrived and when we got back to the hotel Marc said, "Oh, I've got the trunk" and it was made by so and so and everything, and he opened the trunk and there were all these things and then he pulled out a zebra suit, with a tail, you know? The thing is . . . they didn't cut the tail and it was on the ground so when he put it on – 'cos Marc were very small – he forgot that the tail was there and he was swinging about like this, yeah? And, of course, everybody fell about . . . that tail, I mean – it was about two or three foot on the ground. Every time he walked round he was knocking glasses off the table, you know, and I was laughing and Marc turned and picked up his tail and put it under his arm laughing and turned around and said to me . . . "Well dear, that's show business" – and off he toddled.'

PART FOUR

MONOLITH

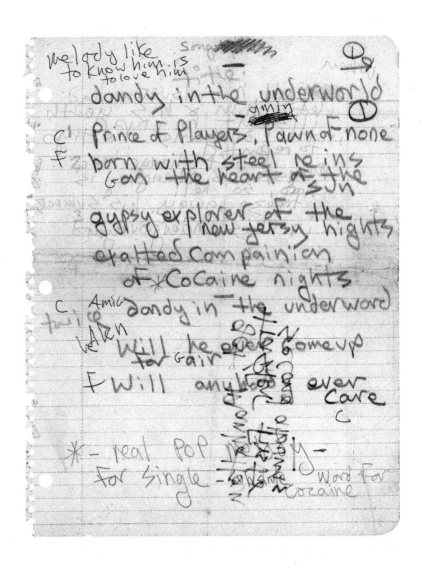

Merciless Minnie stood at the hall
And the elders and fair folk were
beckoned to crawl.
But no, like deep river gods with eyelids of faith,
they dived into eternity.
N.B.
All that lives and ever lived
will be. And will be forever
If you don't shout it out.

From the published 2015 collection of poetry,
Marc Bolan – Natural Born Poet

MEMORIES OF MARC

'I think that most people in the business can't understand me, because I don't fit into any category. I'm a serious musician, but I make pop records. I write poetry and combine it with rock 'n' roll. It was them who created Bolan the cosmic kid or the elfin. Not me. I've remained just the way I always was, so they can't break up the image they tried to create.'

MARC BOLAN

O ver the years, I have thoroughly enjoyed the reflections, stories (some truer than others) interviews, memories and eulogies concerning the phenomenon of Marc Bolan. With the concept of this book very much in mind, I thought it would be instructive to gather as many of these memories as possible, with the addition of one or two surprises and the bonus of hearing genuine fans' memories of those days half a century or so ago.

Dave Johnson is an old friend of mine going back many years. We began talking about Marc Bolan as a gigging artist and recently compared notes on which gigs we may both have attended during the T. Rex years. We were much like two grumpy, confused old geezers trying to recall our youth, our days of freedom, our old girlfriends, or comparing tattoos (I don't have any, but Dave has Marc in the top hat on his arm).

'I went to the Lewisham gig in July 1971,' recalled Dave. 'Croydon, October 1971; Brixton, December 1972; Hastings, July 1975; Folkestone, February 1976; and the Rainbow on 18 March 1977.' The gauntlet was laid down.

'Not bad,' I admitted. Then I reeled off my own gigs: 'Bristol, February 1969; Bristol, November 1970; Devizes, December 1970; Weston-super-Mare, March 1971; Bournemouth, May 1971; Leicester, May and November 1971; the Empire Pool Wembley, March 1972 (both performances); Brixton, December 1972; Leicester, January 1974; Folkestone, July 1975; Newark, February 1976; the Rainbow, London, 18 March 1977.'

While we're both proud of the gigs we attended, both of us feel that the list is rather pitiful and regret greatly that we did not manage to go to more – especially as, at a conservative estimate, Marc Bolan completed in the region of 245 gigs in various incarnations, from the UK to Ireland, Europe, Japan, Australia and the USA!

From the first time I played a Marc Bolan record, I was smitten and became a devout follower. Suddenly there was another human being out there who shared my vision of a far nicer world full of beautiful people, beautiful minds and beautiful thoughts. During the early days of Tyrannosaurus Rex, I simply listened to the albums. My girlfriend's brother was a serious hippy and he would let us sit in his music pit and listen to *My People Were Fair*, *Prophets Seers and Sages* and *Unicorn*. He insisted on three rules. The first was you sat and *listened* (woe betide us if we uttered a sound). Second, we could neither touch the vinyl nor put the arm and needle down on the spinning platter. And the third rule? We could not tell anyone that he was (along with the other older listeners in his room) smoking incredibly fat and long cigarettes. Well, that's what I thought they were at the time!

These visions, drawn and coloured by the sounds that emitted from the record player, took my breath away. I so wanted to be that 'Child Star'. I clearly saw the 'Strange Orchestras', pixies, elves and other magical folk playing bizarre instruments, having a thoroughly good time, drinking dragon mead from angels' trumpets. Then, with all the gathering sated, the 'wielder of words' would arrive to talk of rich historical tapestries, folklore, age and wisdom. The evening sun would then set as the bard sang 'Frowning Atahuallpa (My Inca Love)'.

In February 1969, my girlfriend's brother took us with him to see our first ever gig in Bristol at the Colston Hall. It followed gigs the band had already played that included London, Birmingham, Croydon and Manchester. The countryside flashed by, with us having no understanding of where exactly we were and when we would ultimately arrive, because – being the younger occupants in a typical 1960s love machine (i.e. camper van) – we were shoved right at the back. We could see very little other than when we stopped for fuel or to take a piss as and when instructed. I do recall that the journey seemed to take forever and, by the time we reached the gig itself, I was totally out of it. This may have had a lot to do with the copious clouds of cannabis smoke that circulated around the inner sanctum of the van.

Our weariness was not helped by our being introduced to some weird sounds emitting from an equally weird-looking bloated guitar with an incredibly long neck. I leave it to the legendary John Peel, who was the story teller/poetry reader on that tour, to expand: 'The concerts started with the sitar playing of Vytas Serelis, who, refreshingly, makes no esoteric claims for his music but says, simply, that he plays what he is feeling. In Birmingham, he played for twenty-five minutes instead of his allotted thirty-five, but nobody minded. In the audience were many shining folk with stars on their brows and we've seen them everywhere.'

The only thing I can recall having on my forehead that Sunday was a quizzical frown! I remember some but not all the songs the band played, because – much to my subsequent horror – I fell asleep at some point. Not, I hasten to add, because of the gig: it was more down to being totally fucked. I do remember 'Debora', 'One Inch Rock', 'Pavilions of Sun', but it was not an auspicious start to my gigging life.

Journalist Derek Boltwood summed up what he witnessed that night, noting, 'Marc's songs [. . .] are not involved with very much that goes on outside himself – more a reflection, putting it all in his own terms. He's been involved in the pop business long enough to have learnt to take life on his own terms too, thus the reason for success now I feel.'

'It's a gas,' proudly surmised Marc Bolan: 'I can hardly believe what's happening. We play universities, and on 3 June we are playing a concert at the Royal Festival Hall with Roy Harper and Stefan Grossman. David Bowie will be doing some miming.' A far cry from the words expressed by Marc to Chris Welch in 1968: 'I don't know how big we can get. I just enjoy playing. I play every day and it makes me feel happy. The fact that we are getting paid £150 a gig is a gas. We're not stars or anything, but it's better than starving on five shillings a week.'

In August of 1968, Tyrannosaurus Rex appeared – rather strangely – at a three-day event in Kempton under the banner of the Eighth National Jazz and Blues Festival. Keith Altham who, many years later would interview Marc on many occasions as well as act as his publicist, reported: 'Tyrannosaurus Rex, I felt, were unlucky to be included on an evening which was not really their scene and on this occasion, they were not really mine. Marc Bolan is a clever guitarist and sings mystery songs.' Short and sweet!

On 15 November 1969, it was announced that 'Mickey Finn' would make his live debut as Tyrannosaurus Rex's 'percussionist' on a November mini-tour starting off at Manchester. Finn also did his first radio session on *Top Gear* at the end of the month. With much glee, I also learned that 1970 promised so much more for Marc Bolan. A new album, to be called *A Beard of Stars* – just how cool was that for a title? – was due out early 1970 and the year was potentially flooded with tour dates.

Little was I to know at the time that it would be almost a year into the new line-up before I got to see the Messiah again – 9 November 1970, to be exact. In between my two earliest Tyrannosaurus Rex gigs there seemed few places in which the band did not appear. Bridgend in Wales, London, Brighton, London again at the Roundhouse and, in May, Imperial College, before leaving the UK for the USA. Bedford, London and Dudley welcomed the band back. On 10 October, *NME* announced that the band name was to be officially shortened to T. Rex – although 'Ride a White Swan', released a week earlier, already featured the band's new name – and confirmed the tour dates. That sent this particular young Bolan fan into orbit. The tour was to start on 9 October in Nottingham and – joy of joys! – I would get to see them. Ironically, I was to catch them once more at the Colston Hall in Bristol and (thanks to the new love of my thus-far short life), a special treat to see the band at Devizes the week before Rexmas – or Christmas, to those new to Bolanspeak. Her parents were visiting relatives in Devizes over that weekend and I was kindly invited to go with them all.

The autumn tour started in Nottingham (as already mentioned), and, while I awaited my next gig in Bristol on 9 November, I watched eight gigs come and go. Three more dates then followed before Dagenham on 28 November. This gig had a special relevance because it was here that Steve Currie was first thrust into the limelight as the full-time T. Rex bassist. With him in place, the T. Rex roadshow continued into December: starting in Glasgow the tour closed on the 21st with a gig at London's Alexandra Palace.

In the days when the nanny state was not quite so apparent, I simply sent a note in to my head teacher the previous Friday expressing my mother's regret that I would be unable to attend school on Monday, 9 November, and Tuesday, 10 November, owing to a family illness. Eureka! They bought it, hook, line and sinker! So did I when my mother later learned about my subterfuge – not to mention my apparent ability to forge both her writing style and her signature.

I boarded the train to Bristol Temple Meads station with my girlfriend, her best friend and her boyfriend, who, I must say, I disliked intensely. What a dickhead! Or so I thought at the beginning of our journey to see the Wizard. We arrived at around teatime and, if memory serves, there seemed to be no one else there! After what seemed an eternity (although it was only about ten minutes), in the distance we spotted two young girls and decided to see if they knew where we should be. Did they! The two Bristolian beauties were on their way to Colston Hall as well, so we teamed up and had a brilliant time, comparing notes on fave Tyrannosaurus Rex tracks – not to mention the new single!

We got into the Colston Hall, whereupon the girls all headed off to find the loos. Once they'd done so, they did the most bizarre thing: they went in together. It was one of my many learning curves in a life with women. After what seemed an eternity, the girls rejoined us and we went to find our seats. Disappointingly, we were apparently about twenty rows back from the front, but, once Marc and Mickey arrived on stage, it no longer mattered: a tidal wave of English teenagers descended towards the front of the stage and many stood in the aisles – all very polite at this stage of the emerging rock-god hysteria.

There would be no mistakes from me this time, no falling asleep, no regrets. The energy emitted from the stage, courtesy of Bolan and Finn, took many of us by surprise. It was difficult to keep pace with Marc and Mickey as they danced, strutting backwards and forwards on the stage. All our favourites were there: 'Debora', 'One Inch Rock' – acoustic rock at its finest.

Then the mood changed as Marc plugged in his electric guitar and blasted his way through an amazing set of songs including 'Is It Love' (one of the flipsides of the new single) and 'By the Light of a Magical Moon' – which to this day remains one of my favourite electrified Tyrannosaurus Rex tracks. 'Elemental Child' was exquisite, delivered with passion by a then-out-of-control Bolan – or was that just us? Finally, it was time to say farewell to T. Rex, but not before they finished the evening with their favourite cover, 'Summertime Blues'.

The measure of the man, the monolith, is perhaps best indicated by how fondly the other devotees of the time remember him. Here are some of their own recollections of experiencing the magic of Marc Bolan.

George Underwood – musician and artist, 2017

David Bowie phoned me to tell me that a friend of his has made an album and [was] looking for someone to do the cover. This friend was Marc Bolan. David suggested me and wanted me to meet up with Marc and show him some of my work, which happened a few days later. The meeting was at Tony Visconti's flat in Kensington, London. There was Tony, his girlfriend Liz, David, Marc, June Child and myself. (Steve Took wasn't there – I met him a bit later.) We sat and listened to some rough mixes of the album. I must admit now, although I didn't say at the time, I wasn't that keen on the music. However, the songs did grow on me after a while. Marc was talking about his interests in Tolkien, William Blake, all things cosmic and esoteric. Marc wanted his and Steve's face somewhere on the cover, but, as far as any direction the artwork should go, it was up to me.

I was living with my parents in Bromley at the time, working full time at the New English Library publishers, designing paperback covers, mostly graphics and not much illustration, which is what I wanted to do. Working at home wasn't easy – mostly with a drawing board on the carpet in the living room or the dining table, working into the night! A good friend of mine had given me a wonderful book earlier that year in 1968 – *The Doré Gallery*. It was a massive book filled with the engravings of Gustave Doré. They depicted Dante's *Inferno*, Milton's *Paradise Lost*, *Aesop's Fables* and the Bible stories, all illustrated by Doré. So, when I sat down to get inspiration for Marc's album cover, I flicked through the pages and there were all the stimuli I could possibly want. First it was pencil, which I fixed, and then Indian inks, which went on top showing the pencil detail underneath. Plus, a bit of body colour – probably gouache.

I must say that I was delighted with Tony and Marc's response when they saw the finished artwork. Unfortunately, when I went to pick up my artwork from EMI art department after it had been printed they told me that it hadn't returned from the printers. I knew then that somebody had nicked it, as printers always returned artwork. So, if anyone knows where the original artwork is, please let me know as I would like it back.

Val Slater – Bolan fan, 2017

My very first memory? Hearing a Marc Bolan song called 'Debora' at a school disco when I was about ten years old in 1969. I did not know what he looked like but liked the song. I first saw him when he was on *Top of the Pops* singing 'Ride a White Swan' and instantly fell in love. He had the most beautiful face; he could have been a female model. I was then hooked. When I was younger I had curly frizzy hair and other children took the mickey, but when T. Rex came out I was cool, as I had Bolan-like hair. My bedroom was adorned with posters and magazine cuttings, like lots of other fans I am sure. My proudest possession is a PRS cue sheet, which was for *T. Rex Live in Concert* [the original title for what became *Born to Boogie*]. It is for the script scene 'I look to the left', and is signed 'Marc Feld'.

I first saw T. Rex live at Brixton Sundown. I lived in west London and was only thirteen, so my older brother had to take me as I was not allowed to go over to that side of London on my own as it was a bit rough back then. We got there early, it was 23 December 1972. Everyone seemed happy, as it was nearly Christmas. When the doors opened, we went in and my brother said he would watch from the back but I got to the front and could literally touch the stage. It was all standing downstairs and very dark; I think there was a balcony upstairs. When T. Rex came on I was pushed back by four older boys wearing top hats but I still had a good view. I remember it being so loud and I thought it was amazing. I cannot remember the full set list as it was so long ago, but I do remember him singing 'Baby Strange', 'Metal Guru' (which always sends shivers down my spine), 'Get It On', 'Telegram Sam', and I am sure he sang 'Chariot Choogle'. The atmosphere was incredible, everyone there to see Marc Bolan, and he was totally in control of the audience. To me he was the Wizard, as he made the night magical.

The next time I saw T. Rex was a totally different experience, I still loved them and I was on holiday in Norfolk when I saw a sign outside Tiffany's Ballroom saying 'T. Rex Live Tonight'. I went back in the evening with my boyfriend and we queued up to go in, it was July 1975. It was a lovely evening but did not have the same magic as 1972: there was a different line-up, obviously, and the crowd were not just a T. Rex crowd. Marc broke a guitar string while he was playing 'New York City' and some people started jeering and booing; it was sorted and he carried on. I tried in vain to get a tambourine, as he threw them out to the audience while playing 'Get It On', but never got one. I don't recall the venue being totally full, I think a lot of people there were holidaymakers and it was T. Rex in this venue or Peters and Lee in the venue over the road!

My last experience was when I worked in London. I was with my sister one lunchtime and I was telling her, 'Oh, look, we're coming up to 69 New Bond Street,' which was Wizard publishers, and what I would do if I saw Marc Bolan etc. A burgundy Rolls-Royce pulled up next to us and the door of the Wizard [offices] opened and Gloria Jones and – I think it was – her brother Richard came out and got into the car.

Then Marc Bolan himself came out. I could not believe it. My sister was nudging me and saying go on, go on, at least get his autograph. Marc stood at the door of the car looking at us; he waited for me to approach, but I could not move. I was frozen and literally star struck. It was then that Gloria called him into the car and he got in it and they drove off. As it was London traffic they drove at a snail's pace so I walked along next to the car and he smiled at me all the way down the road and did that little wave he did when he opened and closed his fingers. I have regretted this day all my life, as I was too shy to speak to him. Not long afterwards, he died.

'Memories of God' – Colin Allen, Bolan fan, 2017

[In] 1970 my cousin played me 'Swan' and that was it. Thursday nights were never the same, depending on when *TOTP* was on! Fast forward to 1972, I bought the *[Ride a White] Swan* album on MFP and was knocked out, 'cos I was only aware of singles, couldn't afford much else – until December, that is. 'Solid Gold' battering up the charts and *Born to Boogie* on the cinema circuit. Premiere at Waltham Cross Embassy. Mum took my younger brother to another movie, *The Eagle has Landed* – three hours long! So T. Rex basically babysat me! Oh, deep joy! Christmas [saw more] surprises . . . Record vouchers . . . straight into Studio Records and I wanted a T. Rex album with 'Hot Love' on it. The guy pulled out *Bolan Boogie*. I then clocked *T. Rex*, the album, so I went home with these gems.

In 1977, the year of his death, Marc Bolan's pin-up good looks and endlessly photogenic charisma shone through brightly.

© Bill Orchard/Rex

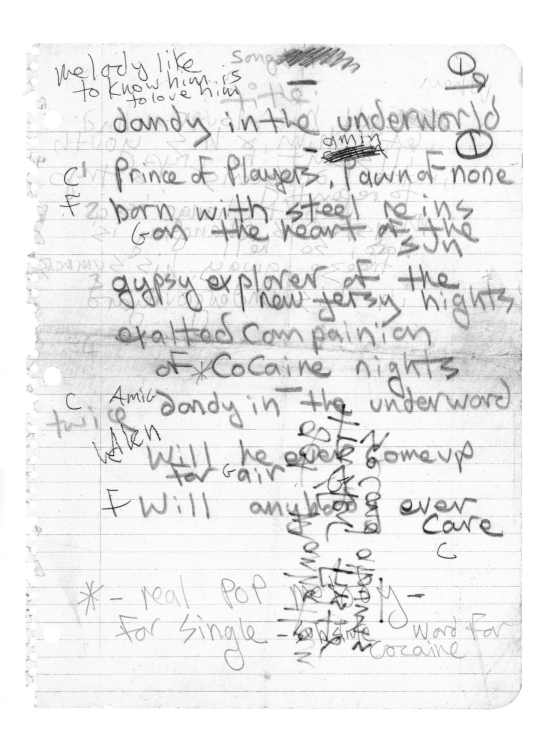

Hand-written lyrics to the album version of 'Dandy In the Underworld'. Upon release, the single had to be edited for radio play to remove the word 'cocaine'. Lyrics reproduced courtesy of Michael Green.

when

~~all~~ all his lovers had
left him, & his youth
i'll spent, he cryp & tryp
to repent, but change is a
Monster & changing is
hard, so he'll
freeze away his summers
in his underground yard

get Manhattan
trashed, first &
Second albums

The reverse side of Marc's original lyrics sheet for 'Dandy In the Underworld'.

January 1976, Heathrow Airport: Marc leaves for the USA with partner Gloria Jones and young son Rolan.

Marc greets some of the fans before a sound check. Gröna Lund, Sweden, 24 May 1977.

Above left: Marc carries out the sound check at the Gröna Lund arena.

Above right and below: Marc in concert at Gröna Lund. This gig was the last live performance Marc made anywhere before he died.

Two sides of Marc on display, as he is captured winding down quietly after his final gig, before getting playful for the camera with drummer Tony Newman.

An original example of Marc's hand-written poetry.

© The Marc Bolan (AKA Mark Feld) Estate

a mansion forged on foundations
~~of~~ of fire, a ~~wh~~ wallet
of indigo & a pitchfork
of camelian gold
where the ~~dying~~ gifts to
me from ~~on~~ ~~too~~ the
bird man of arcadia ~~m~~
~~once~~ ~~once~~ sky/ord in the
~~halls~~ halls of Pan, ~~to~~ ~~the~~
~~too~~ Diamond domed
~~wood~~ Courts, ~~once~~
~~marbled~~ & green have
marbled & green have
long since been ruinous
, the home of the mountain
goat & ~~the~~ winter boys

Above: Another original, hand-written poem entitled 'Dewella'. The poem is reproduced in this book.

© The Marc Bolan (AKA Mark Feld) Estate

Below: A scrawled layout for a live stage set, drawn by Marc.

© The Marc Bolan (AKA Mark Feld) Estate

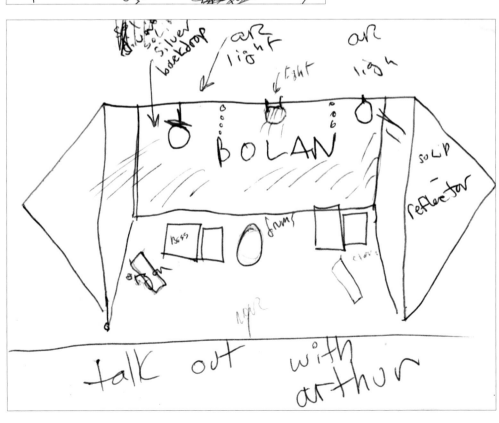

These three photographs, taken in London, are acknowledged as three of the last shots ever taken of Marc. The date is 13 September 1977 – three days before his death.

The whimsical humour, silly streak and visual verve Marc's fans loved him for are displayed perfectly by this shot, taken near Earl's Court in 1977. © *Bill Orchard/Rex*

Marc Bolan:
beautiful dreamer.

1973 *Tanx* – couldn't afford it, so a pools win enabled me to get the first Tyrannosaurus Rex double set. My aunt and uncle got me *Tanx* for Rexmas. New pop show *Lift Off*, 'Truck on Tyke', no Bill. [In] 1974 Dad treated me to *Great Hits* and *Zinc Alloy*. A trip into London got me *Beginning of Doves* and some sheet music. What was Bolan doing? T. Rex finished? What's going on? [. . .] *TOTP* was a crock of its former self!

Come 1975 and *Supersonic*, my memory fails here, 'cos I thought ['New York City'] was the first performance, 'cos I remember putting my hand into the sitting-room light, when it was announced just back from America [or words to that effect!]. Great summer! Paper round paid for other goodies. 1976 was fantastic.

Dad drove me down to London to see 'God' at the London's Lyceum. Wow! Surrounded by like-minded freaks. 'Wahoo.' My dad sat at the back with the *Evening Standard* and earplugs. I got halfway! 'London Boys' and *Dragon*; Boley was back. Rockabilly twats burnt 'I Love to Boogie' – why didn't they buy the left-over stock? It would have sold better! Idiots! Started my first job, in Palmers Green and was surrounded by weird and wacky folk . . . 'Laser Love' got play by Radio 1. That was a trek to Smith's, then a bus ride to Enfield, and another home.

1977 was even better. Marc and Gloria's *Supersonic* debut, Noel Edmonds trashing it. Groove a little pencilled in Ye Gods!! Suit, well the Rainbow, Finsbury Park, bumped into Dave Baldwin and chants of 'Bolan' etc. echoed throughout the station. Somebody predicted it was Bolan's last tour. Couldn't get a beer in the George Robey, so I got one in the Rainbow. Got a 'Half Moon' cut-out, programme and *Dragon* poster, met Jackie Elliff.

The coming months were brilliant: God was back! Talk of a tour later in the year, TV show; two fantastic singles, 'Dandy' and 'Celebrate Summer' from a Bournemouth record outlet. 'Demon Queen' EP, Bolan on Capital [Radio], great interview. Jackie and I were visiting fans in London and it was all good. Then I got two phone calls, which seemed to alienate us all again, pre-1970, when it was announced Marc had died. Nothing was the same. That's it, folks; thanks, Marc, for everything.

'How Marc Bolan affected my life' – Liz Marsden, Bolan fan, 2017

I was always a fan of Marc's, even though my friends were into Donny Osmond or David Essex. I remember seeing an advert in the *Leicester Mercury* that Marc Bolan was coming to Leicester I begged my mum to go. I was fifteen at the time. She said if you can get a friend to go with you, and Dad can pick you up, I'll pay . . . I finally bribed one of my friends to join me.

What a night! After the concert, we went to the stage door first a van pulled up and someone got in . . . we waited, then Marc, Gloria and Mickey got in their car. My friend knocked on the window and cried (as we did, LOL), then my dad pulled up to collect us. As we got in the car he said, 'He's staying at the Holiday Inn' – well, we managed to get off before Marc and made it there first!

My friend and I were waiting by the door as Marc pulled up he got out of his car saw us and laughed I got a peck on the cheek, then he went in . . . oh, how I wish we had cameras. My friend from that day fell in love with Marc [. . .] Sadly [she] passed away two years ago but her wish was to have 'Ride a White Swan' played at her funeral. I always thought I was the only T. Rex fan in the world until Facebook bought us all together and in the last two years since losing my husband my Boley friends have given me a reason to get up every day. I have so much to thank Marc Bolan for.

'Marc Bolan live in Essen, 16 February 1973' – Michael Schnieders, Bolan fan, 2017

My Marc Bolan story started in 1970. Without really knowing, I heard a song on the radio and was immediately fascinated. Because it was an English radio station [BFBS], I didn't know the song title or the artist at the time. In 1971, there was a smash hit on the radio: 'Hot Love', by T. Rex. I really liked that song. Also, the next songs by T. Rex: 'Get It On' and 'Jeepster'. From this point on, T. Rex were my favourite band.

In the summer of 1972, I bought my first album, *Electric Warrior*. The guy at the record store asked me whether I'm a T. Rex fan. 'Yes,' I replied. The guy told me that he had another LP by T. Rex I should listen to. It was *Bolan Boogie*. While listening to the LP, I came across the song that had struck me. It was the song that I had heard in 1970: 'Ride a White Swan'. It was wonderful to find this song. Also, the other songs of the LP were great. I bought also this LP and thus started my Marc Bolan/T. Rex collection.

Then I read in a German music magazine that T. Rex would come to Germany in the spring of 1973 for several concerts, and one concert [would] take place in the Grugahalle in Essen. And Essen was not far from my home town. After I had convinced my parents to let me go to the concert, I bought my ticket for the concert. It took place on Friday, 16 February 1973. Together with two friends, I went from Duisburg, where I lived, to Essen. We [arrived] very early in the Grugahalle in Essen and had to wait for some time until we were admitted into the hall. I had never been to a concert and was therefore excited; also, I would see my idol Marc Bolan live!

The concert hall was full and we waited patiently on the appearance of T. Rex. Then suddenly the lights went out and T. Rex came on stage. The crowd really went wild. After a few seconds 'Chariot Choogle' from *The Slider* started the show. I was speechless. My idol Marc Bolan stood only a few metres away from me on the stage. Unbelievable. T. Rex played all the hits plus songs from *The Slider*. The highlight for me was when Marc Bolan played '20th Century Boy'. This song [was to] be the next T. Rex single and I had not heard this song before. What I didn't know at that time [was that] it was the first time T. Rex [had] played this song live and it was also the only time during the Germany tour. The set list was: 'Chariot Choogle', 'Baby Strange', 'Metal Guru', 'Telegram Sam', 'Buick MacKane', 'Jeepster', 'Hot Love', 'Get It On', '20th Century Boy', 'Instrumental Jam'. There was no acoustic part. It was a very loud rock show.

The concert was over too quickly. It was indescribable. I saw Marc Bolan. And it was a great show. That evening, I swore I would try to visit as many concerts as possible from all [the] following tours by T. Rex through Germany. Unfortunately, this was the last time T. Rex [toured] through Germany. Marc never played any concert in Germany again.

I have still the concert poster, my ticket, some photographs, and the concert on two bootleg CDs in addition to my memories. Even today, when 'Chariot Choogle' starts, I can close my eyes and remember that moment, when Marc Bolan [stood] there on the stage and played that song live. Less than a week later appeared T. Rex [on] the German music show *Musikladen* and '20th Century Boy' was played live. The appearance was recorded two days before the concert in Essen. For me, it is still the best TV performance of Marc Bolan.

I'm still a Marc Bolan fan. I prefer the records from *My People Were Fair* [to] *T. Rex*. But also love the rest of the stuff. In 1992, I was in London and at Golders Green for the first time. [. . .] I will be there in September

2017 to remember the Main Man forty years after his untimely death. My love for Marc Bolan will never end and [I now wear] two Marc Bolan tattoos.

Val Bolan Powell – Bolan fan, in conversation with the author, 2017

When I was eleven, in 1970, I heard my sister screaming at the TV. I looked to see what she was screaming at. On the screen was a beautiful-looking guy with dark, corkscrewed long hair. It was the incredible Marc Bolan singing 'Ride a White Swan'. Wow! From that Thursday evening I was hooked. I became a huge fan.

I was so lucky to see him in concert at Newcastle in January 1974. We were halfway back in the stalls but as soon as Marc came on I felt this electric surge through my body – that's the only way I can describe it. With everyone towering above me, I climbed over the seats to get to the front. Mission accomplished, I found myself looking straight up at Marc. I grabbed the mic stand to get his attention, but the bouncers kept pulling me back. But I just kept on getting to the front! After it was all over, I sat on one of the seats at the front in a daze. As I looked down to the floor, I found a picture of T. Rex that someone else had lost.

My next gig was Sunderland 1976 at the Empire on the *Futuristic Dragon* tour, and then on 10 March 1977 I saw Marc back to his pouting panache best on the *Dandy in the Underworld tour* at Newcastle City

Hall. The gig was simply amazing. I even managed to grab a bit of one of the tambourines that Marc and Mickey used to throw into the crowds – and a bit was all I could expect, as everyone around me clutched for the same tambourine!

To this day I am so grateful that I saw my idol, but tinged with sadness that it was the last time I saw Marc Bolan alive. So sad, so heartbreaking for all of us who loved Marc Bolan. 'Legend' is a word used far too easily these days, but in Marc Bolan's case it is well deserved, as his legacy has stayed the course of time.

'Memories of the Concert 10 March 1977, City Hall, Newcastle' – Michael Green, Bolan fan, 2017

Once the dates had been announced for the tour, I awaited the day the tickets would go on sale. Excited at the prospect of seeing Marc again, I made my way to Newcastle City Hall after school to purchase my ticket and then waited for the night of 10 March to come.

A few weeks later, the night arrived and I had decided to try to smuggle my cassette recorder into the venue. With the cassette recorder wrapped in a thick coat (and looking every bit like a cassette recorder wrapped in a thick coat!), I made my way from Sunderland to Newcastle.

Much to my surprise, I had no problems getting the cassette recorder into the City Hall. Once inside, I remember being surprised at the amount of tour merchandise available. With limited money in my pocket, I bought the programme, sticker and badge, but did not have enough money for the T-shirt (how much I would have loved one of those!). Although it is now well documented that the large circular tour poster was sold at the concerts, I have no memory of seeing them there.

I made my way to the seat (J 31, ten rows back in the stalls) and awaited the performance by the Damned. Having never seen a punk band, or, for that matter, heard much punk music, I really did not know what to expect from them. Having Marc's 'seal of approval' went a long way with me and I enjoyed their performance, with 'Neat, Neat, Neat' standing out as my favourite song.

During the interval, it was nice to see members of the Damned come out to speak to the twenty or so punks [who] gathered around the stage door. Although this concert has often been talked about as being a 'sellout', it was in reality about three-quarters full. It was strange to think that five years earlier – when I saw T. Rex for the first time, in June 1972 – the venue was sold out for two concerts on the same night (a common practice in the early 1970s, when groups generally did very short sets).

At around 8.45 p.m., the lights went down and the room filled with calls of 'Marc! Marc!' broken only by the screams of the adoring fans who had come to worship. Marc walked to the stage and after a few seconds, still in darkness, the opening strums of 'Jeepster' were heard and the place erupted.

The Bolan vibe filled the City Hall air as the new-look T. Rex sounded better than ever with Marc, in his yellow canary-coloured bum-freezer jacket and tight purple strides, looking much better than he had for several years. Gone was the excess weight of the 'Elvis years' [. . .] replaced by the sylph-like physique of the new punked-up Bolan.

After 'Jeepster', Marc thanked the audience for coming and introduced the first of the new songs, 'Visions of Domino', which was then quickly followed by 'New York City' (a truly inspired song that has a mere twenty-seven words but lasts four minutes).

After some retuning of the guitar, Marc chatted to the audience and asked if they liked his new trousers as he turned slightly and lifted his jacket, which brought about the predictable screams from the girls! In truth, Bolan looked stunning . . . and he knew it.

The next song was announced as the new single, 'You Damaged the Soul of My Suit' (which had been an earlier working title for the song), and featured a lovely mid-song guitar solo by Marc. After 'Groove a Little' (and more retuning of his guitar), Marc again chatted to the audience, playfully saying, 'You want to touch me? I want to touch you' to someone near the front. He was obviously in a good mood and enjoying the occasion as much as the fans.

Marc then announced, 'We're going to do one of the old ones for you now – one of the hits,' before launching into a wonderful seven-minute version of 'Telegram Sam' – a song that, to this day, has never dated and remains full of energy. Marc changed some of the lyrics of the song for the live version, notably 'Me I funk but I don't care' was changed to . . . I think you've already guessed it! Before the start of 'Hang-Ups', Marc asked the audience if they were enjoying themselves and mentioned [that he had] a new guitar (a black Gibson Les Paul) and that his old guitar had been stolen.

After more thanks from Marc for people coming to see the show, he said, 'This is the first song I put out. A song called "Debora"' (this was not strictly true, but it was his first notable hit single with Tyrannosaurus Rex). As for the song itself, it was electrified and rocked like a good 'un! As this song was not performed on the French tour of February 1977, I guess this was the first time this version of the song had been performed live. I was pleased that Marc performed it on the *Marc* shows later in the year. 'I Love to Boogie' was introduced as 'My last hit record' and at nearly five minutes long was about twice the length of the original version, though fortunately, like 'Telegram Sam', Marc chose to repeat verses rather than to do overextended guitar solos.

The following song, 'Teen Riot Structure', with its blazing mid-song guitar solo, sounded so good, and, for me at least, was probably the best of the new *Dandy* songs heard that evening, though I felt spoilt for choice as *all* the new songs sounded wonderful. For 'Dandy in the Underworld', Marc kept in the line 'exalted companion of cocaine nights' (it would later be rerecorded for a single release with 'cocaine nights' being [changed to] 'T. Rex nights'). When the first verse was repeated in the song, Marc [again] used the line 'exalted companion of my cocaine nights' – was there ever any doubt about this song being autobiographical?

For me [. . .] 'Dandy in the Underworld' [. . .] is Marc at his lyrical best and remains one of his greatest songs. This song, and there are many other examples on the *Dandy* album, shows how far Marc had travelled from the lyrically weak offering of '*Futuristic Dragon*' just a year or so earlier.

A relatively short (three-and-a-half-minute) version of 'Hot Love' followed with the band then leaving the stage. After a short while the band returned to the stage for the final song, a thirteen-minute version of 'Get It On', which for me is my favourite Bolan song of all time, partly because it was the first T. Rex single I bought and, I guess, was the catalyst for my becoming a life-long Bolan fan. Although it was always great to hear Marc play 'Get It On' live, I feel that [. . .] he could never improve on the released version. The original 1971 version with Marc's laid-back vocal delivery, Tony Visconti's lush production and Ian MacDonald's sax is simply unsurpassable. As with previous live versions of the song, Marc's guitar went into overdrive – though, fortunately, no whips were involved this time!

T. Rex performed the final song without any involvement from the Damned. At the Portsmouth gig ten days later, [however], the Damned would join T. Rex on stage for the encore, possibly indicating how much Marc had enjoyed working with group. As T. Rex left the stage, the fans started to filter out of the City Hall with smiles on their faces and, based on this performance, with the knowledge that T. Rex were still very much a force to be reckoned with.

As I reached the foyer there was some commotion as the merchandise stall had started to sell copies of the *Dandy* album – the day before it was officially released! Lack of money became a problem again and I dashed out of the City Hall to get some more money from my parents, who were waiting in the car park opposite. Once I had the money for the record I dashed back across the road and into the foyer – only to see the last few copies of the album being sold. The disappointment of not getting the album did not diminish the pleasure of what had been an incredible night. Bolan and the new-look T. Rex of Dino, Herbie, Miller and Tony had given an awesome performance. Marc's belief in the new *Dandy* songs was obvious – never before had he performed so many new (and previously unheard) songs live in concert in the UK.

Just prior to the concert, I had a feeling that this would be the last time that I would see Marc [. . .] This had nothing to do with the sad events that would follow in September, but much more to do with the changing landscape of the music scene. This was early 1977 and the punk/new wave movement was gaining momentum and threatened to make the old wave look 'tired'. Much to Marc's credit, he fully embraced the punk movement and, possibly uniquely, he was the only established artist to invite a punk band to tour as a support act.

Seen in the context of the time, this was a very brave move on Marc's [part]. Remember that this was just over three months after the infamous Bill Grundy/ Sex Pistols incident on the *Today* show, which resulted in the Sex Pistols being banned from virtually every town in the country. For most people, their only exposure to punk rock was via the coverage of the Sex Pistols in the tabloid papers. Marc looked beyond the tabloid headlines and saw a movement, which was fresh and exciting.

Before the concert, I harboured thoughts that Marc may not be around in a year or two's time. Those thoughts evaporated during the concert as T. Rex pumped out one great song after another. Would I get to see Marc again? Of course, I would – wouldn't I?

'Diaries of a Teenager' – Mercedes Sullivan, Bolan fan, 2017

Thank goodness I kept a diary in my teens – my memory is rubbish! Some things I do, however, remember very clearly. Everyone's living rooms were brown, school was boring but we had to go so that we could earn our treats: youth club, records, crisps on the way home from school, magazines, music papers and concerts!

My two older sisters smelling of patchouli and my mum shouting at them to wash it off all the time. Looking forward to Thursday and *Top of the Pops*! Listening to Bob Harris, John Peel and Annie Nightingale on late-night radio.

My sister and I went to many concerts together, but our favourite group was Tyrannosaurus Rex [and T. Rex] but my most vivid memory of seeing Marc on stage is the charisma he oozed, a tiny figure on the edge of the stage who filled the entire venue with his awesomely beautiful persona. From the frantic strumming on beautiful ballads like 'Girl' and 'Spaceball Ricochet' to the exciting and powerful 'Elemental Child', he left me mesmerised and the feeling of euphoria stayed with me for days afterwards. I couldn't concentrate on schoolwork or anything else, couldn't wait to get home to listen to his records whilst reading and memorising the lyrics and drawing his face on bits of paper.

The early 1970s [were] without doubt a wonderful time for music and live gigs in London and I wouldn't change any of it for the world. I just wish it [hadn't] ended . . . I thank Marc Bolan for helping me escape what was the humdrum, boring life of school, family arguments and general dreariness of real life in my teens and helping me find myself. The magic of his music has stayed with me throughout the years and now at the age of fifty-nine I still love and miss him. But his music lives on and always will.

'My last meeting with Marc' – Kathleen Heron Andryszewski, Bolan fan, 2017

I first became aware of Marc Bolan and T. Rex at the age of eleven years, when 'Hot Love' was playing on the radio, and have been a massive fan of both the early Tyrannosaurus Rex onwards ever since. I first saw T. Rex live at Newcastle City Hall in 1972 at the age of twelve years [. . .] to this day I do not know how my parents allowed this.

There were two concerts on the night. I attended the early one. This was the most amazing experience. In those days, there was no ordering tickets on line, it was a case of getting up at the crack of dawn to get the first bus to Newcastle. I remember hitching a lift on the milk float. There were thousands of fans who accumulated around the City Hall in the hope of getting a ticket. I remember it was front-page news. The street was closed off and the police were brought in to control the crowds. It was mayhem! The anticipation and excitement that followed during the countdown to the concert, and then finally seeing and hearing Marc live, was a blast.

My friend Judith Henderson and I continue our friendship and love of Marc Bolan to this day. [. . .] We were both lucky enough to attend another three live concerts in '74, '76 and '77. We would always arrive at the venue on the day early in the morning to sit at the stage door in the hope of seeing Marc arrive for rehearsal, which he always did. He was usually surrounded, but we managed to get a few pictures each time. I have fond memories [of] meeting and chatting to fans – and not so fond memories of freezing to death in my little satin bomber jacket. Don't think Fenwick's department store were so happy about us pouring glitter in our hair in the middle of the shop, either. At the Newcastle concert in 1977, we met a guy called Yinka Sobo (I think this was his name – so many years ago!). He told us that his mum was Rolan's [Marc's son's] nanny and gave us a photo of his mum with Rolan and the address of Marc's office on New Bond Street. Unfortunately, the photo was stolen from my car with my briefcase in 1978. I also recall at Newcastle, think it was '74, a security van being reversed into the side doors and all the members of T. Rex were locked inside before the van moved off. We were all surrounding the van and pulling at the door when it flew open. Mickey stood up and was kicking everyone away whilst he pulled the door shut. They all appeared quite startled [. . .] I would imagine [it] was quite a frightening experience for them at the time.

In September 1977, Judith and I visited London to stay with family friends. We were heading for New Bond Street with the intention of meeting Marc. We would get up each morning and sit outside Marc's office. There was a café next door with tables outside, so we would sit there each day with the table as close to the door to Marc's office as we could. [. . .] On 13 September, [we looked] up to see the most beautiful sight ever walking down the street towards us: there was no missing Mr Marc Bolan floating towards us with his pink satin Marc jacket and red trousers.

Marc was so lovely and let us snap away taking photos. I remember him commenting on our accent and noting that we were from Newcastle. He went into the office but said if we hung around he would come back down. Don't think there was any decision to make there, then! He came down a while later with a woman and they went in to the café. Judith and I decided, for some ridiculous reason, not to follow him as we did not want to invade his privacy too much – although we were bursting to do just that. Wish we had done so – maybe we could have had more conversation with him. I think we were just in shock that he had turned up and just totally spellbound by everything.

Other fans then arrived who we had met on other days who ran [or were] involved with the fan club. They told him they were planning a party for his birthday. Marc said something like, 'I'll have a word with Mickey and may come along.' Judith and I arrived home in Morpeth on 15 September full of our stories of meeting Marc and dying to go to the photographers in the morning to put our films in to be developed. No instant photos in [those] days – you got your prints a week later.

I was woken in the morning of 16 September by my mam. I knew she was about to give me bad news by the look on her face. Nothing could have prepared me for what she said. Devastation was an understatement. I cannot describe my grief or disbelief at what had happened. I remember Judith and I crying all the way to the photographers and begging them not to lose the film. We did get our lovely photos developed from that day, which have been our treasured possession since that day.

I did lend out the negatives a couple of times to other fans and only found out a few years ago that they had been circulated on the Internet around the world. I was shocked to learn this, but happy that these pictures are shared among fans as they are likely to be the last taken of Marc alive. I had no hesitation in allowing [John] to use a few in *Beautiful Dreamer* [. . .] to share yet again with all those who remember Marc Bolan so fondly.

We now live in a world of the Internet and social media and this has introduced me to many lovely Marc fans who have become my friends. I am looking forward to the fortieth anniversary Bops and remembering the man who [has been] a massive influence in my life since the age of eleven years and continues to be a part of my life here and now.

'That night in Watford, 1973' – Bari Watts, Bolan fan

[Bari Watts – long-time Marc Bolan fan and himself a musician – reminisced to Keith Sinclair, who runs the ELO Beatles Forever tribute site, about a special night.]

If I had seen the advert for this gig [ELO at Watford Town Hall in April 1973] to be honest, I probably would not have gone, as I was not an ELO fan in those days at all, really. A mate and I went to gigs in and out of London together a lot and sometimes it would be a gig we both fancied and other times we would just tag along to each other's choices. He said to me, 'Fancy going to the town hall tonight?' so I asked who was playing. When he told me it was ELO, my face dropped, but, as I said, he often came to gigs of my choice and, as Watford Town Hall was very close to where we both lived, and we used to go there a lot anyway, I reluctantly agreed. So after sitting through the entire ELO set – feigning interest – the set finally ended (I can't remember if there was a support act).

Then, Jeff introduced a very special guest and on swaggered Marc Bolan! For the first time in the entire evening, I woke up! I had been into Marc's music from early 1968 (I still am) and the last time I had seen him play live was, I think, at the Lyceum in late '71, just when his pop stardom really started to happen – so let's just say I was a tad happy! They launched into a rock 'n' roll medley, which, to my memory, included 'Roll Over Beethoven' and, although it went on for some time, for me it was not nearly long enough! Marc was really into it and did his whole rock 'n' roller routine and it was just marvellous. I've heard there was apparently some dissension from a section of ELO fans, but, to be honest, from memory, I didn't witness it myself. Everyone seemed to be really into it and enjoying themselves, almost as much as Marc was! This was, sadly, the last time I ever saw Marc play.

I was, and still am, heavily into the Tyrannosaurus Rex and early T. Rex era of Marc's music and I think, when he became a very big star, I kind of felt that it had all moved on to a new, younger generation. I think we all experience things like that. Something [that] you naïvely think is 'yours' suddenly becomes 'public property' – but, on this occasion, it was great to see him strutting his stuff again!

Anyway, years later in 1985, as a sound engineer, I was working on the soundtrack recordings for a stage musical. On one of the sessions I had ELO bass player Mike de Albuquerque in, laying some stuff down on the show tracks (one that I played guitar on). During the sessions, we spoke about the Watford gig briefly and Mike said that he personally wasn't 100 per cent aware that Marc was going to appear, although Marc had been in the studio with the band on earlier dates and it was a possibility. He did say that he really enjoyed Bolan's presence there that night, though. I wish I could remember a bit more of this gig, but it was a long time ago!

Alistair Shield-Laignel, Bolan fan, 2017

Discovering Marc Bolan created my ongoing love and fascination for music; I know without him my life would have been poorer. My mother was a big Mario Lanza fan and [to her] that was 'real singing', not like those 'long hairs in their scruffy clothes taking drugs'. Had she known my babysitter once played the whole of the Beatles' *Abbey Road* LP to me, she would have been, shall we say, rather cross!

When my mother was out I used to listen to my brother's Kinks and Rolling Stones singles he had left behind when he went to university. My friends would come around to join in as well and that led to the discovery of Radio Luxembourg. [After] purchasing a cheap transistor radio with my pocket money, I used to listen under the bedsheets at night to avoid detection.

One day I switched on and a song had just started. It was frenetic and hooked me in instantly, loving the strange voice rising above the hiss, crackle and pop. I had just heard Marc Bolan for the very first time performing 'King of the Rumbling Spires'. Nobody at school had heard of this Tyrannosaurs Rex or Marc Bolan so I was there at the beginning, before any of my female classmates put his poster on their wall and declared undying love!

I wasn't allowed to buy records and had to listen out for Marc on the radio. I clearly remember hearing 'Ride a White Swan' and going around singing 'da-da-dee-da-da . . .' to the point I got a detention at school for doing it in class. Finally, I purchased my first record and it was the legendary MFP *Ride A White Swan* LP (mottled buff edition) complete with the Paul McCartney quote about T. Rex being the new Beatles. Made me proud, because I had begun to think of Bolan in an 'imaginary brother' sort of way. The LP was played to death, eventually sticking and jumping on several tracks. I still have it.

Marc was my hero; embarrassingly I even bought the occasional *Jackie* magazine, pretending it was for my sister, to get the latest information and photos. Such dedication in the time of skinheads and 'bother boys'. I never wavered and even with the rise of Slade and Doc Martens among my peers, I stayed loyal. Mind you, it was fortunate I was a big guy. It is still hard to describe the feeling when you got your hands on a new Marc item and it still happens today. I would spend hours in those early days looking at every minute detail, which led to the unearthing of the run-out groove messages – which were of course just there for me!

My best friend's sister loved Marc for a while and she gave me the 'peace patch' poster with the orange background when her alliance switched to David Cassidy. It was on my wall for years, eventually falling to pieces.

When seemingly everybody else started wearing Bowie T-shirts, there I was standing out in my Bolan ones. I didn't realise at the time how fickle the music business was and could not understand how anybody would think any other artist was better than Marc Bolan and not like him. To my shame, I once wrote a rude word next to Bill Legend's name on my copy of *Slider*. It had just been announced he was leaving T. Rex and to a young uninformed mind that was a big sin. Thankfully, I had the chance to apologise to Bill when I met him years later.

THE GREAT AND THE GOOD ON MARC BOLAN

'All Marc knew was how to create and play.'

JUNE FELD

One can scarcely overstate the impact on rock-'n'-roll culture and aesthetics, as well as the influence T. Rex's music, energy and charisma has had on other musicians – an influence which was only really acknowledged after Marc's death. With this in mind, the following pages of the book are devoted to testimonials and interviews with other musicians on the subject of Bolan.

'I still possess the ticket stub from my first-ever concert, T. Rex at Belle Vue in Manchester, 1972. I wore a satin jacket, very high-risk situation in Manchester city centre.' – Morrissey

'Anyone who can write "I ain't no square with my corkscrew hair" is OK by me!' – Adam Ant

Excerpt from interview between the author and Mickey Finn in 1991

John Bramley: At around the time of *Electric Warrior* you then had the phenomenal success with 'Hot Love' and 'Get It On' and 'Jeepster'. By then, had you got used to it? Did you think that 'We're getting what we set out for'? Were the surprises beginning to diminish for you?

Mickey Finn: No. That's a very good question. Do you know what? The funny thing is, I didn't have a target. I mean [. . .] T. Rex for me, personally speaking [. . .] was like being on a roller coaster and we were just whizzing along – you know – and at times none of us knew where we were going, but wherever it was it was good. And I was having a good time. Great relationship with everybody and happy. So, I don't think it was a conscious target. I don't think even Marc even knew!

JB: OK, that leads me on to something else: June Feld. How important, how influential, do you think June was to the way Marc behaved or responded to all those events in the early days?

MF: Well, let's start by just saying Marc owed a lot to her. She was brilliant. She kept all the business together. I mean . . . I can give you one great example of how good she was. Being me and Marc – this was early days and we're doing a university or a pub, right? – and they had these big bouncers on the door and Marc used to say to June, 'You know we broke the percentage, go and get the cash' – you see, it was all pound notes in them days, you know. And June used to just – bold as brass – go in there and she used to come out and count it and say, 'That's the percentage.' And she was great. And she handled the business, worked out the money, you know, filled the car, made the phone calls, and meanwhile Marc totally relaxed and wrote his music. Other bands were having hassle with the management and especially with June going in there – 'cos she's a woman! – she took all that worry away from him, you know. I mean, it's very unusual for somebody to get a wife to be able to handle that side of the business and to live together.

'I learned how to scream from Marc Bolan.' – Joan Jett

'It was like being jealous of your best girlfriend. He had everything – the hair, the eyes, the makeup, the glam. The worrying thing was you did kind of fancy him, being this feminine-looking guy. But then you had the music as well, both things together, and the combination was unbelievable.' – Cilla Black

Excerpt from interview between the author and June Feld in 1991

John Bramley: There's a wonderful story that Mickey Finn was telling us about how all the other bands were having problems getting the money from [JF laughs] the gigs and there was little June who used to go in and you'd come out counting the notes and all the other bands would say, 'How the fuck did you get that? How did you do that?' Did that ever scare you, with what you had to do, or did you just find it a dead easy thing to get on with?

June Feld: No, it was – it was my due [laughs]. I mean: they did the work, I collected the money. And I wouldn't broach nobody. I mean, I got money out of them, the horrid management, who looked like gangsters, who had these sort of nightclubs. And Marc and Mickey would go and do the thing and then you'd have this huge man and you'd say, 'Oh, I've come to collect a hundred pound' – whatever it was – 'a hundred and twenty-five pounds.' 'Oh, you've got to go and see "Thing".' So you'd go and see 'Thing 2' and 'Thing 2' would send you off to go and see another "Thing".' But I got it – and I got better at it. I mean, you only had to go and see one 'Thing' eventually [laughs], instead of going down three or four. And I always got the money. Always. I never once – ever – was knocked for money from them.

JB: How did Marc come up with the concept of the glitter and glam? Was it a very conscious move of Marc's – did he wake up one day and say, 'I know what I'll do . . .'?

JF: No. Never. It happened totally by chance – um – in a *Top of the Pops* studio. [. . .] We'd gone through the Anello & Davide strap shoes because I used to wear them [and I bought some for him] and I bought some glitter, which I had in my handbag in a little tube that you put on Christmas cards – you know, when you put glue on Christmas cards and then you chuck all this stuff over it and tip it off and you've got a nice pattern.

And I said it would look really, really nice because I'd recently seen a very good mime artist, friend of David Bowie's called Lindsay Kemp, and I'd been about the week before to see Lindsay and he was dressed up as a clown and he had glitter teardrops on his face – just one, two there – completely white-faced – he was bald – very beautiful mime, his body, very articulate, and just eye makeup and these two tears. And I said to David, and to Lindsay [. . .] 'God, that's beautiful' – because it lit up in the lights when his face was so white [. . .] and so I pinched the idea and I bought this stuff that I used to put on Christmas cards and went to *Top of the Pops* and said to Marc, 'Just let's try it.' And so I had a little glue because – as you see – I bite my nails, but I used to wear false nails in those days because it looked glamorous, and I had nail glue and I got a toothpick and just drew the glue on like that and said, 'Just tip your head back' and poured the stuff on and then [tipped] it forward and hit the back of his head. And there it was: a tear drop. That was the first time. [. . .] And from then it just went crazy.

[Author's note: the story has always been that it was the wife of Tony Secunda who came up with the idea of the glitter on Marc's cheeks.]

JB: Having started that and having had the idea of the glitter and the paraphernalia of glam rock that followed, do you think Marc ever looked back on it and regretted the glam?

JF: No, absolutely not!

JB: No, I mean did he enjoy it?

JF: No, I mean it was just a progressive thing, really. It was just another dimension to what he was doing. And anything he did was like that, it was just like another layer on another layer on another layer.

JB: Don't you think, as I have often reflected, that it became an out-of-control monster?

JF: That's a very good question . . . I think he felt it became a monster when there were millions of people all covered in gunk [laughs] whizzing about the place with feather boas and strap shoes and things like that. But one can't do anything about it then.

[I then suggested to June that – in the words of Oscar Wilde – 'Imitation is the sincerest form of flattery that mediocrity can pay to greatness.' I added, 'And let's be honest, Marc was the original and therefore the greatest.']

JF: The strange thing about Marc was that he always was an insular person. The fact that he could go out and put on this huge persona – I mean, you could put him into a room not when he was Marc Bolan, 'rock-and-roll star', [but] when he was Mark Feld, 'lad', and everybody would be aware of him. Now, he wasn't six-feet-five tall – he was *five*-feet five – and a little scruffy little thing – but he had an aura about him and he could walk into a room and he'd sit down and if you . . . I don't know, if you ever noticed about him, he never did

[his] shirt sleeves up, he always turned them back so his wrists were visible. Currently it looks awfully camp [laughs] but it wasn't. And he sat in a chair and he was totally aware of himself. And I think he was born like that, because when I met him, when he was very young, he was totally aware.

'He was one of the few British pop stars who didn't play safe. He wanted to play on our side, not theirs. He always believed in a second life, so he'll probably be back again.' – Billy Idol (Generation X)

'Marc was one of my few true friends. We always lived close to the edge when we were together. He was a star in its truest sense and I will miss him more than I can say right now. But my thoughts now are with Gloria – that she will get well again and with Marc's family. Their loss is the greatest.' – Steve Harley (Cockney Rebel)

Herbie Flowers Q&A (abridged)

There are many Bolan (R)experts today and one of those is John Wass, whom I have known for some years now. During a conversation, I asked him if he still had the interviews he did with Herbie Flowers, Dino Dines and Tony Newman, all members of T. Rex's last line-up. All the questions John Wass asked them were submitted by members of the 'T. Rex' and 'Till Dawn' memberships. The interviews were all conducted in 2003.

Herbie joined the 'new look' T. Rex in September 1976, around the time of 'Laser Love', and stayed up until Marc's death in 1977. With such a varied career, a Q&A session with Herbie was bound to be interesting!

John Wass: Herbie, can I start by asking you, how did you get involved with T. Rex?

Herbie Flowers: Marc phoned me one day – in '75, I think – just to do a few recording dates, which I enjoyed immensely. He also used Tony Newman on [drums]. Dino and Miller were already doing stuff with him. Then a few gigs popped up, a tour of France, a TV series entitled *Marc*. All good. But because the work was intermittent, and anyhow I already was doing lots of freelance studio and live work, there was no way I, or Newman, would ever give all that up just to get wages for each thing that popped up. With a growing family, not an option. Plus, I'd not long spent some gruelling months on the Diamond Dogs tour and had developed tinnitus. Plus, an opportunity to help put Sky together was on the cards. More suited to my ambition at that time – something different, a chance to do a bit of composing, a share of the profits, trips to Oz, Japan, NY, take the family . . . who wouldn't?

JW: Can you remember your first T. Rex session?

HF: One phone call. At AIR London. Twenty-five pounds plus five pounds porterage. Can't remember the four tracks we did in three hours, but they were all one-takers, I think, and they were put on *Dandy in the Underworld* as far as I know. We worked quick. That's my job. Didn't wanna be hanging around all day in studios. Still don't.

JW: Did you have any input on sessions, or did Marc have everything worked out beforehand?

HF: Nothing to work out, really. If it was four bars of E on the guitar then I'd played four bars of E on the bass. If the guvnor said, 'That's not working,' then we'd try something else. All Bolan's pieces are a doddle to play.

JW: Apart from the bass, did you ever contribute any other instruments? Ever got the chance to lay down a tuba solo for a T. Rex song?

HF: No, of course not. I'd save my tuba playing for 'Grandad', Blue Mink's 'Banner Man' and Lou Reed's 'Goodnight Ladies'. T. Rex was pure rock music.

JW: Is there a favourite track or session you played on?

HF: 'Heroes' on the last *Marc* programme. David Bowie was on it, and in the dressing room he asked me what key his masterpiece hit recording was in. By accident I said E instead of D. A simple mistake, but nonetheless it sounded brilliant. Hope David doesn't think I did it on purpose . . . That was the last time I saw Marc, I think.

JW: How did you rate Marc as a musician and a boss?

HF: A star. Nice player. Great to be with. Never once saw him lose his rag, ever. I think we supported him well by not influencing him badly. Now I think about it, what a great band that was.

JW: Were you on a set wage and did Marc pay the going rate?

HF: Of course. Wouldn't and couldn't have it any other way. All the songs were his, the show was his. Everything was how he wanted it to be. So why should I expect any more? People ask if I feel bitter about only getting a session fee for playing the bass on Reed's 'Take a [sic] Walk on the Wild Side'. Nope. A bar of C and a bar of F for four minutes. Not my song. My job.

JW: Did Marc ever rib you about 'Grandad' keeping 'Ride a White Swan' off the No. 1 spot?

HF: Only once. Hard luck. Rolf Harris's 'Two Little Boys' kept 'Banner Man' off the No. 1 spot the following year. And I'd played on it.

JW: A favourite T. Rex tour?

HF: All of 'em. Tony Newman was/is my best friend. Everything . . . everything, made us laugh. Still does. The two biggest flannellers in the business and we're still going strong. Him in Nashville touring with the Elderly [Everly] Brothers, Crystal Gail, John Prine, etc., despite a quadruple, and me, here, packing my suitcase to go and do a week's workshop at the Conservatory of Music in Helsinki. Paradise.

JW: A favourite T. Rex moment?

HF: In a Little Chef on the A1 at one in the morning after a terrific gig. A coachload of us, including the damn Damned, all starving hungry. [Music agent] Tony Howard rang the bell and asked the proprietor and his wife if they'd open and cook us all a full breakfast each. You'll have to help, said the proprietor. So we did, including the coach driver. The two loos, like all loos, had great echoic acoustics, so we had a rude noise competition. Whoever could make the loudest raspberry by blowing in the inside part of the elbow would win. Tony Newman won, hands down. At least fifteen times louder than Rat Scabies. I was second.

JW: What made Marc get back into shape again?

HF: Willpower, love, being a dad, and a belief, perhaps, that he had the light to enrich all of our lives. That he certainly did. More people I've met in my travels as an itinerant musician ask me about Bolan than all the other so-called artistes put together. What was it like working for him? Fine. I shall always treasure knowing him, loving him and all those around him. He knew exactly what he was doing.

JW: What did you think of the *Marc* shows?

HF: I was very happy with it. Being a bass player, there's not a lot to do except sit on the beat. So, I could look around at the punters. Their faces said it all. He had a magical effect on them all. If people don't like T. Rex (Bolan, that is), there's something wrong with them.

JW: How do you look back on your time with T. Rex?

HF: Those years weren't my best years, for my own reasons. But, yes, it was good. I don't rate myself too highly in the grand scheme. I was just a middle-rate busking jazzeroonie, and still am. For every hit I've played on there are a thousand that weren't – a lot of which I might have been responsible for fucking up with [my] out-of-tune, busy, in-yer-face style. Can't bear to hear myself on any of it. So now you know.

JW: What is your lasting impression of Marc?

HF: How tiny he was. Beautiful. Think how much he gave us all in this hot, demoralised society we've nearly demolished.

'I would dream of being a rock star who dressed like Marc Bolan, walked like Jerry Hall, and had the panache of Ginger from *Casino* and the mystery of Isabella Blow . . . Glam culture is ultimately rooted in obsession and those of us who are truly devoted and loyal to the lifestyle of glamour are masters of its history. Or, to put it more elegantly, we are librarians.' – Lady Gaga

'You'll find T. Rex in many groups making records now,' says Bolan's erstwhile producer, Tony Visconti. 'Even U2 copied Marc a little bit. His music was 1950s-based, and he found a way of polishing that sound and making it fresh and timeless. There was some magical thing that he tapped into. You can't make a better rock-'n'-roll album than *Electric Warrior*. We were inexperienced, had no safety net and Marc was at his best. He was the most focused artist I've ever worked with.' – Tony Visconti

Dino Dines Q&A (abridged)

John Wass: How did you get into the music biz?

Dino Dines: I always wanted to be in a band – local

bands, then professional, lots of knocking on doors, lots of gigs, hard work.

JW: At what age did you start to play keyboards. And are you classically trained?

DD: I started on keyboards at about eighteen. I first played guitar at thirteen but had a banjo at four. Mainly self-taught, a minor amount of formal classical training.

JW: What did you do before T. Rex?

DD: Many bands, the most famous being the Keef Hartley Band, P P Arnold, the Hollies – too many to mention.

JW: How did you get involved in T. Rex?

DD: Recommendation by Mick O'Halloran, Marc's roadie. He was once a roadie for P P Arnold.

JW: Where did you get the name Dino?

DD: Given the name at about eight years old by a schoolfriend.

JW: Can you remember your first session with the band?

DD: Paris some time in 1974. I did two tracks on clavinet, I can't remember the track titles.

JW: Initially, was Marc after a full-time keyboard player?

DD: As far as I know, Marc was looking for a full-time keyboard player.

JW: Which were happier times: *Bolan's Zip Gun*/ *Futuristic Dragon* or the *Dandy* recording sessions? And which album do you prefer?

DD: I enjoyed all of my time with T. Rex. But

the happier times, without a doubt, were the *Dandy* sessions.

JW: Did you have any input on sessions, or did Marc have everything worked out beforehand?

DD: Most of what I did was my own idea. Tunes were never totally worked out. Marc would come into the studio with a basic idea for a song, more like a sketchbook to be finished in the studio. Sometimes I would go to Marc's house and we would work on tunes together.

JW: What is your fave T. Rex line-up?

DD: Rainbow gig line-up. Marc, Miller Anderson, Herbie Flowers, Tony Newman and of course me, Dino Dines. What a great rock-and-roll band that was, a privilege to have played in that band.

JW: Which is your fave track that you played on?

DD: 'The Soul of My Suit'.

JW: How did you rate Marc as a musician and a boss?

DD: Great rhythm player, one of the best. Not so good at solos. He always treated me as an equal, I never saw him as a boss, so I suppose that makes him a good boss.

JW: A memorable gig that sticks in your mind?

DD: The Rainbow – a great gig. All the press came to see the band fail. The band did not fail – quite the reverse, in fact.

JW: What did you think of the *Marc* shows?

DD: I thought they were fine, [but] on the wrong time of day. They gave many bands exposure and that's good.

JW: What's your lasting impression of Marc?

DD: I liked Marc a lot, he became a good friend. He was very talented, a true star. He could be a so-and-so at times, but so can we all.

[Sadly, Dino passed away in 2004. This was his last printed interview]

'The first time I ever got laid was after a Bolan gig (she had corkscrew hair, glitter under her eyes, stars on her cheeks, satin jeans). Phewee!' – Paul Morley (*NME* journalist)

'Even people who didn't care for his records acknowledged his charisma.' – Rosalind Russell (*Record Mirror* columnist)

Tony Newman Q&A (abridged)

John Wass: My first question for you is this. Marc was often slagged off by critics for his musicianship. A question I'd like asked is what musicians, like you, thought of Marc as a guitarist/musician?

Tony Newman: I thought Marc was a great musician. He had a good groove, was a really good guitarist.

JW: Any funny/memorable stories from the *Marc* shows?

TN: The funniest moment I remember with Marc was him falling off the stage on the TV show after his duet with David – that was funny.

JW: Any memories of the last-ever T. Rex gig in Sweden?

TN: The gig in Sweden was cold, but the audience was warm.

JW: What are some of your memories of the *Marc* shows?

TN: Great, great fun. I don't remember a bad show. Marc had wonderful charisma.

JW: Did Marc and David perform a full song? I read that Marc was really upset that one of the takes hadn't been videotaped!

TN: Marc and David did perform a full song.

JW: How did T. Rex get on with the Damned?

TN: I always took the piss out of the Damned, and would announce them on stage as 'Not everyone's cup of tea – the Dimmed.' Great pals, we became.

JW: If you had one lasting memory of your time with Marc, what would it be?

TN: The last of the great pop stars. Full of colour, charisma, joy and showbiz to the max!

'[Marc Bolan] was the one who started the ball rolling again, and it's always nicer to associate yourself with the first. There I was just gawking [at Wembley], 'cos I loved him up there. He's exciting and just to see all those people dressed like him again . . . I mean, it's the same trip.' – Ringo Starr on *Born to Boogie*

'It has been a long time since I have interviewed anyone with the kind of mental sparks that Bolan is spilling out in all directions and a long time since I have heard such good sense. It was something of a revelation to listen to this apparently placid, cherubic-looking figure in his blue romper suit, red-and-yellow-hooped jersey, adorned with a "Derek is Eric" button, spill over with enthusiasm for his new scene.' – Keith Altham

June Feld on Marc's Music (in conversation with the author)

June Feld: That's where he was. He wrote words – very beautiful words that he put to music. He didn't write music and then put words to them – he used to come home and say, 'But they didn't really hear the song.' Therefore, at the gigs, everybody in the band, they all whack up the volume. You'd get Steve on bass and it would be up at number ten, and Marc's guitar – it didn't have twelve on the knob, but if it had it would have been up at twelve; and the drums were turned up and so they just played louder and louder to overcome the audience reaction. Not to overcome, just to make themselves heard above it. It's the price you pay, I think, for that sort of fame. Listen to his words, because his words were very beautiful.

'There were times, especially in the early, early years, [Marc] used to be a very affectionate and you knew, you felt that he cared for you. And I always remember that little tweaky smile of his – you know – and he put his arm round you [. . .]

207

and that was lovely – you know, you felt that you belonged. It was a [. . .] nice vibe that he gave. And I always remember that little smile of his, yeah. And he'd sort of twist away with his head and shake his hair. Yeah, it was great.' – Bill Legend, 1991

June Feld on 'Spaceball Ricochet' (in conversation with the author)

June Feld: 'Spaceball Ricochet' is a wonderful story and [the actual story] came as a title. It didn't come as a song, initially. [. . .] When we lived in Clarendon Gardens, we lived [in] the upstairs of the house – we had the two floors. In the basement of the next house was a housing trust and a little boy lived there with his mum, and it was a one-parent family, which there weren't that many of in those days. [His] father was black and his mother was white, so he was this most beautiful child. Golden brown but with white-blond hair, curly hair. And he really got on well with Marc, 'cos Marc had curly hair, and so they were like sort of positive and negatives – wonderful. And he was called Anton.

And one day he came and his mum had obviously gone up and got her dole money and her giros and things and she went to Woolworth's and bought him a pair of, um, baseball boots. Nowadays they're called Converse and children spend forty-five pounds on a pair. These were nineteen and eleven [2.5p off £1]

208

[. . .] in old proper money [laughs] – in real money – in real terms. And he was so proud of them and he had little, like, tatty old shorts on and a T-shirt and these gleaming baseball boots and he came and bashed on the door and – 'Marc! Marc!' [. . .] I went down and let him in and he whizzed up the stairs, hared up the stairs – you know – leapt up the stairs and he said, 'Look what I've got, Marc. Look what my mum just got me – I've got Spaceball boots,' and he proceeded to run across the drawing room, up the wall, like two or three steps and he would ricochet off that wall, whizzed up to the other side and then ricochet off the back. [. . .]

And he was just whizzing backwards and forwards and Marc went 'Hm, "Spaceball Ricochet",' and he wrote the title down and then [. . .] they had a cup of tea and, you know, played records and hung out, and then Anton went home for his tea, and then Marc was gone. And he was upstairs and [makes sound] that's how it came about. [. . .] And lots of people think it's autobiographical, and it is, but it started off from Anton, who was a little boy with his new Spaceball boots.

'Whoa, whoa, you can't use that riff, that's fucking T. Rex.' – Paul 'Bonehead' Arthurs (founder member and rhythm guitarist of Oasis), on hearing Noel Gallagher's opening chords to the song 'Cigarettes and Alcohol' for the first time.

June Feld on 'Hippy Gumbo' (in conversation with the author)

'I don't think anybody ever in the whole world would guess,' June Feld replied after I had asked her which of Marc's own singles was his favourite. 'It was "Hippy Gumbo".'

John Bramley: Oh really? Why?

June Feld: It was made – well, as well you know, a very long time ago. It was when he was very young and he thought he was homosexual [. . .] and he was in love with a man. I mean, in fact, Marc wasn't homosexual. He chose to play that role to the media later when David Bowie did his bit about it and it became peer-group-cool to be gay or to be bisexual – whatever one called it. [But] he was very young – he was about fourteen or fifteen and he was very in love with a man [. . .] a very nice man – and he wrote this song and if you listen to the words [. . .] – it was about a person that was looking at his reflected image [. . .] and one of the lines is that 'his face and mine were mine'. That they were one, in fact. So all the things he was feeling were, in fact, inside himself. And the fact he took a gun out and shot him – but what he did is, he shot himself. And that was his favourite song [. . .] many years before I knew him – and I think it was a time when he was very alone [. . .] and the only way he could express himself was through his words.

He wrote constantly. He was never given deadlines – things like, '[You] need twelve tracks for another album' – because he probably had forty-eight songs written. Whether they were good enough to be recorded – I mean everything he wrote was perfect – [but] from his point of view. It took people like Tony Visconti, and me and – I mean those sorts of people that knew him very well to be able to say, 'Well, look, they're all great but [. . .] these are [. . .] the sunshine bits, these are the "golden things"' – and that [was] fine and then he'd say, 'Yes.' He never worked on them again. [. . .] Once he was happy with it, that was it. It wasn't that arduous process of going back and reworking it and rewriting it and . . . I mean, the only other thing is that he may have written a new middle eight – [rather] not a new middle eight, an additional bit to – to slot into it.

'I would have been about eleven when I first heard this ["Metal Guru"]. T. Rex were the first band I was a fan of and Marc Bolan was my hero at the time. As a song, it's quite nonsensical, but that doesn't matter: a great record doesn't necessarily have to be a great song. Once you've been affected by any art in such a powerful way, it stays with you.' – Johnny Marr

PART FIVE

'I COULD WRITE A BOOK ABOUT MY LIFE

Like a husk it seemed to me that I,
Dove danced upon the sea
My heart of winds blew wild and warm
Night fleet, foot fled before my storm,
A dawn of pinks and azure blue
Flowed like faith, all on the few,
Who virgiled thru' the vaulted night
Free of the falcon fools of kite.
Who ride the skys in ships of ice
And eat the frozen hearts of lice
And bed in sheets that the whiprworm spun
And hide 'neath our lys from the light of the sun

From the published 2015 collection of poetry,
Marc Bolan – Natural Born Poet

MARC BOLAN
IN HIS
OWN WORDS

Tragically, Marc was taken from the world before he had the chance to write a book about his life. Yet his words were widely recorded, and we can glean much from them. Marc was often quoted saying some of the most outlandish things. As June Feld told me many years ago, this was how he was: 'He was unaware that what he was saying was impossible, logically or otherwise.'

Is this necessarily a bad thing? Not really. Why should it matter? I had always looked upon Marc as a Tolkien disciple. As far as I am concerned, as a lifelong fan, I enjoyed this side of Marc Bolan the most – after his music, of course. Marc had this dreamlike persona that you could always detect in his mannerisms. And his face? It told you more about him than words ever could. Throughout his career, he did nothing wrong (in my eyes) when it came to his songs and lyrics. And as for his poetry? Well, that took a little longer to digest, for many different reasons. For Marc Bolan, a born wielder of words, simplicity was never an option. It was only as I grew up, constantly revisiting his poetry, that it began to dawn on me that I was simply tapping into a head full of mythical words and enchanting dreamlike images.

Musically, there was little difference in a perverse kind of way. Marc had no boundaries. I would argue that Marc lived his life thinking and dreaming outside of the box. Every chord he played was in harmony with the effect he wanted to enlighten us with.

'I use music to express myself,' he acknowledged, in many articles. All his efforts were to bring about good old rock 'n' roll with a sprinkling of the Bolan magic. Marc believed in himself without question – and who can argue with what he did in his pursuit to be acknowledged as a serious lyricist or, as he often would refer to himself, a bard?

'I believe that all my lyrical ability was learned in a past life as a bard,' he told *Beat Instrumental* in February 1971. 'Songs are now much more basic than ever and the lyrics are also becoming more economical. I'm sometimes a bit self-indulgent with words,' he admitted. 'Sometimes I write purely for me but there's more than me in this world and I should try to reach them.'

In November 1971, Marc told *Beat International*'s Steve Turner that part of the inspiration for 'Jeepster' lay in the 'use of a word that sounded nice and the use of a surrealistic imagery. Jeepsters apparently look as good as the word sounds, so that the lines "Girl I'm just a Jeepster for your love" paint a nice Dalí-like picture in your mind if you allow your imagination enough freedom.'

'Music is a great soother,' Marc went on. 'It's the only physical high I have.' Of some of his new songs he said, 'There's an easy-to-grasp feeling about them.'

Marc wrote 'Mambo Sun' for a six-year-old girl who lived in the flat below him. (Sample line: 'I got a powder-keg leg and my wig's all pooped for you.') 'She laughed so much when she heard it,' the singer remembered. 'It was the way the words popped and moved. If I'd have sung the "Scenescof Dynasty" to her she'd have gone out and played Frisbee or something.'

Marc was in conversation with Steve Turner again come October 1972, but it is clear that Turner was not keen on the new direction that T. Rex were then taking. He was challenging, scathing even to the point of patronising the success Marc was having with the songs on *The Slider*. 'I find your lyrics less "story-like" than they used to be,' he told the singer. Marc responded by suggesting that in his own opinion, the world has changed: 'I feel that what a poet should do is write down what there is.' The interview continued:

> Is there a pheasant crescent moon, then?
> 'There was when I wrote that song, yeah.'
> Does it fill your toes with rain?
> 'I got soaked when I was walking home from the Speakeasy.'
> Do you think that somebody hearing that song would immediately say, 'Ah, he got soaked on his way home from the Speakeasy?'
> 'I don't care! . . . You can only do what you do.

I mean, when Dalí paints a painting he doesn't think about what Edwin Hawkins [the leader of a gospel group who had a hit in 1969 with "Oh Happy Day"] will think about it. Seriously . . . I mean, you'd never do anything!'

In 1969, Marc spoke to an uncredited journalist: 'I've been writing since I was about fifteen, I suppose. I started out with poetry and then I got into music. But I've been the same. I didn't want to be a soloist. I didn't want a four-piece band. I didn't want an electric scene, you know . . . Poetry is poetry and songs are songs. I wouldn't write words and put music to them. Words I can write all day. I could sit down and write the words just off the top of my head because that's what it's like inside that. I'm very prolific – I'll write perhaps two songs a week.'

Any artist will tell you that their latest offering is the best they have done thus far. Marc Bolan was no different in this respect. As I read over what he had to say to various music hacks about his own material, one line kept recurring: 'This is the best one yet.'

'Success, although at first seeming like a reward,' suggested Turner, 'must soon become a taskmaster necessitating that a certain standard be reached with all the songs.'

'Success encourages me to be a better craftsman,' responded Marc. 'I dig lyrically what I'm doing now. Emotionally I'm more into it.'

Many of Marc's associates have declared that he was impatient in the studios – both with them and with himself. This, I would venture to suggest, was a sign of an artist who constantly found himself living on the edge of the next song. 'I've never felt so insecure or such pain as I do now with my music because I am so exposed,' he told Keith Altham in April 1971. As many other artists who have graced our musical history also found, you are only as good as your last hit single or album.

'Being a much more aware person than a lot of people credit him for,' surmised Penny Valentine in a *Sounds* piece in October 1970, 'Bolan concluded that it was all very well going on about elves and woodlands and forest gods but that this only endeared itself to a minority audience.'

'All the T. Rex heads loved it and so it was totally right,' Marc admitted, 'but certainly for the mass media it was totally wrong – they just couldn't relate to things like that in the musical setting we were providing . . . in a harder tighter musical sound it seems to appeal to them much more . . . "Ride a White Swan" is doing amazingly well . . . we added electric guitar and a heavier feeling into the backing.'

'One of Marc's qualities is that he's always been a very prolific writer,' conceded another journalist, Caroline Boucher, for *Disc and Music Echo* in December 1972. 'He's still got about fifty songs from around the *Electric Warrior* era that never went down on album.'

'Mickey always reminds me of them because I gave him tapes of them and sometimes he'll sing one and I'll remember,' Bolan told Boucher. 'There's already too much material for the next album unless we do a double album, which I don't want, because I've never found one that was satisfactory.'

Armed with that magical thing called hindsight, I regret that I didn't read the music papers during Marc's zenith. I had plenty of friends who would tell me when he was on tour, when new singles or albums were coming out, and little else mattered. So I never saw the following self-penned article that he put together for *Disc and Music Echo* paper in 1974. What I like about the article is the rawness: it is Marc speaking free from interruptions by the interviewer. It flows, and displays some barbed but genuinely heartfelt reactions from a singer tired of the constant suggestions that he was a spent force, scathing in response to the ways of media manipulation and what was expected of him by some of his fans. I hope you will find it as fascinating as I did. It is unedited.

'My name will live on . . . I'm a lifestyle'

Disc, 1974

by Marc Bolan

I've been in the business seven years now and during that time I've had to take an awful lot of slagging but let it be understood – it's gonna take a hell of a lot of brain washing by the media to get rid of me – Marc Bolan! It's a nice idea for artists to be allowed to write their own columns occasionally, because you get the chance to talk about things that are important to yourself. Like, this month is a pretty important one in my life, because I'm going back out on the road to face British audiences again after two years. I know a lot of my fans have thought that I've neglected them, but

I really don't think I have, because there was 'Born to Boogie' for one thing and plenty of singles and albums released in that period.

Just now I'm busy planning the tour, which is gonna be quite a thing. I sat down the other night to write out a list of the songs I wanted to play and ended up with more than 40 of them. What I'll do is play a bit of everything ranging from the early days to a medley of hits and about three or four of my new songs, which'll be featured on my new album 'Zinc Alloy . . .'

Later this month my new single 'Teenage Dream' will be released. I cut it in America some time back and to be honest I reckon it's one of the best singles I've done. 'Truck On', I must admit, wasn't one of the Bolan greats, but it was still a good single. The band we've got together is a pretty incredible one. There's Carmen's drummer Paul Fenton specially joining us and I'm bringing in two sax players, two chick singers as well. Now, we're still getting everything together. We're a lot more visual these days and a hell of a lot more violent and I think we're gonna give a show that won't be beaten this year by any band. The Pink Floyd's lighting engineer is now working for me and his ideas are lavish I can tell you.

I don't know what kind of audience to expect, but I guess they'll be the same fans as before. They mustn't expect to see the T. Rex they saw in the past because now we're completely different. I decided on a change when I was in America and now we're extremely funky. I know that, barring a few tickets the whole tour has sold out, which obviously pleases me and I'm told the kids who are buying the tickets are between 12 and 17. It proves that I'm not in the same kind of bag as Donny [Osmond] because his audiences start from about the age of six upwards.

My fans are the most important thing in my life, but they must dig me for what I'm doing. I don't, and never have, gone out of my way to please them. I stopped playing in Britain because there were so many other things to be done – like taking on America for instance. The lack of British appearances and the changes I made when I was touring in other countries did me a lot of good, and now I'm really looking forward to playing again. I've not gone out of my way to buy special clothes for this tour or anything like that. Now Marc Bolan is Me and whatever I give comes naturally. I've changed . . . I really have! David Bowie used to have to change clothes about 25 times during a performance. Gary Glitter must dress himself all up, but I don't have to do it. I've always been aware that I owe everything to the kids and for that reason I always try and please them in any way I possibly can. They look upon me as being a glamorous pop idol and that's what I try to be. But understandably there are times when I feel out of my head and physically and mentally worn out, and when I get like that, I don't want the kids to see me.

After this tour, I'll be blasting back to the States, and there's the Bolan solo album and possibly a few solo concerts after that. I've been thinking for a while now about gradually phasing the band name of T. Rex out, because that's really where I'm at. Now it's me with a few backing musicians and that's how the whole Bolan thing should be developed. Perhaps later, I'll do concerts backed by strings and various musicians who want to work with me as I want to work with them.

You know, even before I entered the music business, I quite expected all the fan adulation that I've received over the last few years. Mentally I was prepared for the things that happened before they did. I don't have time anymore to think, 'WOW! I'M MARC BOLAN'. I honestly don't know what it's like to be Marc Bolan. I believe the ultimate star is the star who makes it by just being themselves. Rod Stewart is an example. I mean he really likes football and that kind of thing. I'm just as people think I am, as well. I'm all things real to those who dig me.

Money! You know I've made a hell of a lot of the stuff, but I never think about getting it, but I do think about keeping it. I'm a business man – but there again I must be. I employ a lot of people to work for me and their livelihoods are upon my shoulders. The office I'm writing this from in Bond Street costs me thousands.

I never really socialise with other people in the business apart from my own set. I don't function very well when I lock myself away in my house and try and get things together. I must exhibit what I feel within my own surroundings and that helps me build the confidence I need to take my music and ideas further.

I know that nothing is lasting and I don't deliberately go out of my way to plan things for the future. Bolan is alive today, but he might well get knocked down by a car tomorrow and that would be it. Who knows what's gonna happen tomorrow anyway? I could lose all my money, and the thought of that doesn't particularly worry me. I wouldn't be happy being penniless – I do like luxuries, but it wouldn't break my heart. I guess my name would live more than just a record. I'm a lifestyle. But Marc Bolan does go through a lot of personal emotional type things, but I don't think I should lay my problems on my fans. Kids must moan about something, so why shouldn't they moan about me sometimes. When I don't play gigs for a long time they are entitled to moan, because they aren't aware of what I'm trying to do.

I know a lot of my fans think they created me, but they didn't. Everybody goes through changes, me included, and as opposed to being created, you just grow and mature as you go along. I've done enough to never be forgotten. Well time's running short on me again, so I guess I better wrap this up. I hope you enjoy reading my ramblings. Look forward to seeing you during the tour. Be writing to you again. Bye.

*

'I feel very directly involved with woodland spirits. I accept that trees have souls and lives and that man was once a very splendid beast – he is no longer, but there was a time. An elf to me is not someone who's that big. It's a man that's perhaps eight feet tall with silver hair and can control his mind in a way that's a good thing. I don't see that all people have imagination.'
MARC BOLAN

Talking to *ZigZag* in March 1970, Marc revelled in the story of his time in France and his meeting with a wizard ('Walking in the woods one day I met a man who said that he was magic' – 'The Wizard'). 'I lived in a forest for a while, and then in a chateau with this cat who was a magician,' he told *ZigZag*. 'He wasn't a black magician; he was very aware of the workings of the human mind ['Knew why people laughed and cried' – 'The Wizard'] and the elements. He had very many old books about control of environment by thought projection, and he could transmit feelings so that you understood what he meant implicitly, which is magic to me ['Wonderful things he said, pointed hat upon his head' – 'The Wizard']. It was a yoga magic rather than one involving sheep sacrifice at midnight on Glastonbury Tor ['Why they lived and why they died' – 'The Wizard']. It was very nice to be around someone like that.'

It is a typical Marc Bolan story, full of passion, wonderment, mystic – and with tongue very firmly in cheek. 'He came back from France where he claimed he'd met this wizard in the woods and lived with him for three months and learned his magic spells,' remembers Simon Napier-Bell. 'In fact, he'd been for a weekend package tour and met some gay guy. But Marc was a great fantasist and, in the end, he believed he'd met a wizard. But the great thing about him was that if he knew you knew the truth he'd have a laugh. I said, It's just some bloke you met in a gay club, isn't it? Marc said yeah, but he could do conjuring tricks. Marc got this reputation for being precious but he wasn't, really. He was always funny with his friends.'

What I failed to grasp while following Marc as a teenager – or perhaps 'failed to appreciate' would be a better way to phrase it – was that, far from the frivolous, tongue-in-cheek beautiful dreamer, he was as much a political animal as others around him at the time. 'If there's anything I can do to put society in the right direction I'll do it,' he told Keith Altham in 1972. Altham himself concluded that, 'Marc feels that by being given a certain position as a musician he is also able to help society.'

Bolan's political side was never truly picked up on and there were very few political statements or messages in his lyrics until, of course, along came 'Children of the Revolution' with only one line needed to guarantee the song's immortality: 'I drive a Rolls-Royce, 'cos it's good for my voice'. Subtle yet powerful. Of course, there is a twist of irony here, in that Marc Bolan never learned to drive! 'There have been incidents where I have gone out for a drive in the car and crowds have surrounded it and blocked me in. Very close to riots.' He told Altham, 'I never understood why people had dark windows in cars. I do now. There are times when attention can be fun. I end up signing autographs and talking about music . . .

'You might get some guy coming up to you that wants to smash you one. That's why I don't believe there is security. You could die tomorrow, you know. So, I try to live today,' he mused. 'I never know when I may die . . . I'm obviously not going to be changed because of the success; I haven't been so far. I'm an honest person. At the moment, I feel periods of great energy and periods of great weariness.'

Marc frequently found himself having to defend his words and was challenged by more than one journalist about his statement that he had proved that a normal working-class guy could aspire to owning a Rolls-Royce. 'I just happened to say Rolls-Royce in the instance you're quoting because people respond to it,' he argued. 'In a song I've got coming up I sing, "I drive a Rolls-Royce 'cos it's good for my voice", which is the campest thing of all time, but I just felt that it was how jive those things are.'

'I suppose I'm a sort of teenage idol but I'm not a teeny bop idol,' Marc insisted to Keith Altham in 1972. 'I'd be very upset if the press wrote me off as anything less than a musician and a poet.'

To him, there was privilege in being a rock star. Musically, politically, sociologically, Marc was able to absorb so much more through his experiences, and, as he stated, 'Exploration is very important. I've been round the world twenty-five times faster than anyone else.'

'We haven't much time to say what we want to say,' Marc told *Beat Instrumental*'s Steve Turner in 1971. 'The walls of eternity are closing in on us. I mean, whatever has to be done, has to be done within the next ten years.' The singer clearly felt that the Earth was in trouble on so many levels. It is a shame he did not have more of a platform, or at least I did not think enough credence was given to tell us all what he thought.

The fun side of Bolan manifested itself in many different directions, as I hope I have already shown. His seriousness was frequently held in check by his gift for self-deprecation. 'I take my music seriously and my writing seriously, but I'm not serious about the fantasy,' he stated. 'I've always been a bit of a wiggler. I just dig dancing. It was a bit difficult to wiggle when I was sitting on the stage with Peregrin Took, otherwise I'd have been up in those days.'

'I'm my own Captain America,' he told Robin Smith of *Record Mirror* in 1977. 'My life has been brash and colourful and I find myself identifying with superheroes. *Electric Warrior* was the idea for a comic, but it never took off.'

'I still want to be known as a showman and poseur, but I also want people to take me seriously,' he revealed to Caroline Boucher of *Disc and Music Echo* in December 1972. Boucher added, 'After a few years of talking regularly to a guy you begin to think you know him, but then you touch on a subject and down come the shutters, and with a jolt you realise you just know a friendly person who'll talk for hours about music. He won't talk about the magician he used to live with in France before he first joined a group "because it's not relevant to pop music".'

'The four years from when I was fifteen were formative and I loved and enjoyed them,' Bolan admitted, 'but they mean no more now than remembering the smell of the wood burning on bonfire night.'

Marc Bolan, columnist with *Record Mirror*, 6 August 1977

I'm back on the Box (as the pic on the News Page proves – just regard it as a little bit of early Joan Crawford 'Hooray for Hollywood'). You can get your details on the Dave Brown pages – he of the perpetual Status Quo T-shirt. However – just in case he has made room for one or two other totally unworthy items – about Rotten, Bowie, Zep, Jam, the Stranglers or similar unknowns

– I'll bang my own gong a bit and fill you in on the biggest news since we exclusively revealed that Kermit the Frog was gay. My own TV series is something I'm really excited about. It came about because Granada's big chief Johnny Hamp wanted someone to host a rock show which would bridge the gap between today and tomorrow and generate a genuine feeling for young people. Someone who would be accepted by the new wave, the old wave, super-nova, black holes in space and skateboarders (more about that little explosion later).

Anyhow when Muriel Young asked me to do the shows I was straight into the idea. There are one or two people who have the wrong idea about Mu, just because of her early love affair with 'Pussy Cat Whilem' [sic]. I think I should be honest – most of us early boppers used to fancy her like mad and Wally Whyton was a total wipe-out. Basil Brush was just not my kind of fox.

BUBBLES

Mu [Muriel Young] languishes under one of those heavy titles: 'Head of Children's Entertainment', but she is also a very bright lady with a clear view of what you want. It was Pussycat Whilem's [sic] keeper who put Mike Mansfield in charge of the programme which launched The Rollers on 'Shang a Lang'. This enabled Mike to fulfil his destiny on 'Supersonic' and bury the likes of me up to me earlobes in foam, balloons and bubbles to bring back real fun and fantasy into those tired old presentations on early Top of the Flops.

229

Mu booked the Jam, on the kids 'Get It Together' prog six weeks before their 'In the City' hit the charts. She has her eyes and ears wide open for new wave talent. While we are on new waves, old waves and punk I think it is time to take a stand. New wave and punk are just words thrown up by the media to bag a new generation and some fresh energies. But I am getting sick of some of the moronic, talentless new groups joining the bandwagon, after it has rolled past, with nothing to recommend them but the age-old ability to join in after it's too late. So, from here on I am drawing the line between the punkoid junk, and some of the stupid violence that accompanies it, and genuinely talented people with something new to say. The Pistols, the Stranglers, the Jam, the Damned, the Clash, Generation X and the Boomtown Rats fall in the talented category.

OPTIMISTIC

New bands like Boomtown can hardly be bracketed in that high adrenaline new wave category, but I've seen them twice at London clubs and they have the ability to become huge. These are the kind of groups I want to get on the show but they are not the only ones. Others I would like are: Gary Glitter, Frank Sinatra, Vera Lynn, Steve Harley, Elvis Presley, Parliament, Pat Boone, Kermit the Frog, Rolling Stones, Iggy Pop, David Bowie, Batman and Be Bop De Luxe – though this may be a little optimistic.

The dust being kicked up by the new wave is resulting in the spitting out of groups like the Pirates, who don't pretend to be teenagers but are homed in on the new energy levels (along with bands like Burlesque and solo singers like Elvis Costello – both are getting into this re-energising). Watch them go – watch them grow and, if you care, just call them new and leave the mindless, bovver boys, who have made 'punk' a bad word covered in their own gob, to their own devices. I'm sick and tired of punkoid junk but into new wave funk. So now you know what to expect from me on my new TV series – I want the Jam, the Stranglers and the Damned, plus the best of the old wave. We won't have any corny hyped-up studio audiences, just plenty of imagination and fresh ideas. So far none of the names I have suggested for the show have been turned down by the Granada bosses.

My new T. Rex single 'Celebrate Summer' has a very definite new wave feel about it. If anyone thinks it is deliberate they are quite right. I know a good thing when I hear it, and am young enough to enjoy adrenaline-rush rock. On TV I intend to do it against the background of a genuine skateboard team called 'The Benji Boarders'. I hope you'll feel I'm moving with the times 'cos I gave up doing re-make of Sun record oldies with 'I Love to Boogie'. If you like the one – wait till you hear the one I've got in mind for the TV theme tune.

Let's rap a little about skateboarding which, not too many of our older administrators seem to have realised, is going to be the new recreation for the young. I doubt if one local council in 10 is thinking about tracks for skateboarders, even though you can hardly walk along the pavements for them. Skateboarding is already a monster sport in America. Over here the only contribution I've heard of local officials making was to spread gravel over a park to stop kids doing it. What we want are proper skating areas. All you need is a banked rink, you can rent the protective gear for this healthy sport that'll keep you trim, outdoors or in. Given some rock and roll music to move to, you've got the best combination since surfing and the Beach Boys.

Some oldies were drumming up publicity to prevent the punk and ted war, which never existed until they publicised it. They'd have done better to donate funds to this new sport. I still get letters asking about some of my early partners like Steve Peregrin Took from the Tyrannosaurus Rex days and Mickey Finn from T. Rex. Steve's writing songs – he sent me some tapes recently and they sounded interesting. He turned up to the T. Rex concert at the Rainbow, and we still see each other now and then. He left me because he wanted to get into a heavy rock band.

Mickey Finn has an antique business and is about to become a dad. There may be a possibility of my working with him shortly, on his own single.

Finally, some random ramblings. I dropped in by sheer accident to the Jam's celebration of their Hammersmith success and met Mum and Dad Jam, Mr and Mrs Weller. Mum was a particularly nice lady and very concerned about her son's future in the business. They have their heads well screwed on so there is no real need to worry.

Ran into Bruce Welch of the Shadows at another party. He admits the Shadows recent re-union was pure nostalgia for him and the audience, unlikely to produce a regular re-grouping. Bruce is a very honest guy, unaffected by the business and he's become a force in the songsmith stakes. He's no mean producer either . . . my manager, Tony, asked his four-year-old son who he would rather see on my TV show – The Rubettes or Johnny Rotten. Guess who he picked? Rotten is a star like it or not. Don't believe all this old crud about them not playing on their singles. Steve Jones is a damn good guitarist. We're still sifting your suggestions about your favourite made-up group. Next time you see me it will be Marc-the-shark-on-the-box jaws with a guitar, smiling like Peter Frampton but still trying to be flesh and blood for you.

APPENDIX A
MARC BOLAN GIGOGRAPHY (1965–77)

Although once or twice Marc was known to shake things up a little, the sets were reasonably rigid. We would love to hear from anyone who can add to the sets listed below, or inform us of variations on any gigs Marc undertook.

1965
19 November: London, Wembley, Empire Pool. The Glad Rag Ball. *Marc's first known live appearance. Three songs were performed.*

1967
JOHN'S CHILDREN

10 March: Leatherhead, Surrey, Bluesette Club
24 March: London, Oxford Street, Tiles Club. Support to the Easybeats.

German tour support to the Who. John's Children played five concerts on the tour, between 8 April in Nuremberg and 12 April in Ludwigshafen, before being thrown off by The Who's management.

8 April:	Nuremberg, Germany, Messehalle
9 April:	Wuppertal, Germany, Thalia-Theater
10 April:	Herford, Germany, Jaguar Club
11 April:	Dusseldorf, Germany, Rheinhalle
12 April:	Ludwigshafen, Germany, Freiderich-Ebert-Halle
26 April:	Leatherhead, Surrey, Bluesette Club
29 April:	London, Muswell Hill, Alexandra Palace, The 14 Hour Technicolor Dream
3 May:	Leatherhead, Surrey, Bluesette Club
19 May:	Beaconsfield, Buckinghamshire, Youth Club
24 June:	Warminster, Wiltshire Football Ground

TYRANNOSAURUS REX

21 July:	London, Tottenham Court Road, The Blarney, UFO Club
22 July:	London, Covent Garden, King St, Electric Garden
27 August:	Woburn Abbey Festival (unconfirmed)
23 September:	London, Covent Garden, Middle Earth. Support to Denny Laine's Electric String Band

Set list:
1 HOT ROD MAMA
2 SARA CRAZY CHILD

3 SCENESCOF
4 HIPPY GUMBO
5 GRACEFUL FAT SHEBA
6 HIGHWAYS
7 THE WIZARD
8 MUSTANG FORD
9 THE LILAC HAND OF MENTHOL DAN
10 THE BEGINNING OF DOVES
11 CHILD STAR
12 DWARFISH TRUMPET BLUES
13 KNIGHT
14 CHATEAU IN VIRGINIA WATERS
15 PICTURES OF PURPLE PEOPLE
16 LUNACY'S BACK

7 October: London, Covent Garden, Middle Earth
24 November: London, Covent Garden, Middle Earth
22 December: London, Kensington, Olympia

1968
12 January: London, Covent Garden, Middle Earth.
                     Support to the Nice and Limousine
26 January: Southampton, Southampton University.
                     Support to Pink Floyd and the Incredible
                     String Band
23 February: London, Covent Garden, Middle Earth.
                     Support to Blossom Toes and Fairport
                     Convention
9 March: London, Covent Garden, Middle Earth.
                     Support to the Jeff Beck Group

236

21 March:	London, Royal Albert Hall, Imperial College Charity Carnival. Support to Donovan

First headline gig for Tyrannosaurus Rex:

5 April:	London, South Bank, Purcell Room. Oak, Ash and Thorn
13 April:	London, South Bank, Purcell Room. Oak, Ash and Thorn
13 May:	London, Covent Garden, Middle Earth. Supported by Junior's Eyes
18 May:	Southampton, Southampton University. Support to Captain Beefheart and His Magic Band
19 May:	London, Covent Garden, Middle Earth
22 May:	London, Covent Garden, Middle Earth
25 May:	London, London School of Economics
3 June:	London, South Bank, Royal Festival Hall. The Babylonian Mouthpiece Show
15 June:	Birmingham, Birmingham University
17 June:	Sheffield City, Memorial Hall
23 June:	Birmingham, Erdington, Mothers
29 June:	London, Hyde Park, The Cockpit
6 July:	Woburn Abbey, Bedfordshire. Woburn Music Festival
9 July:	London, Covent Garden, Middle Earth
24 July:	London, Havestock Hill, Country Club
10 August:	London, Sunbury-on-Thames, Kempton Race Course. Afternoon performance
10 August:	London, Chalk Farm, Roundhouse. Evening performance

24 August:	Limburg, Belgium. Jazz Blizen
31 August:	Godshill, Isle of Wight, Hayles Field, Ford Farm. The Great South Coast Bank Holiday Pop Festival
15 September:	Birmingham, Erdington, Mothers. Support: Bakerloo Blues Band
20 September:	Nottingham, Albert Hall
27 September:	Billingham, County Durham, Technical College
28 September:	Malvern, Winter Gardens
29 September:	London, Haverstock Hill, Country Club
2 October:	London, Leytonstone, Red Lion
5 October:	Glastonbury, Somerset, Town Hall
12 October:	Norwich, University of East Anglia
18 October:	Beckenham, Kent, Mistral Club
9 November:	Birmingham, Erdington, Mothers
21 November:	Manchester, Free Trade Hall
23 November:	Chippenham, Neeld Hall
1 December:	Cambridge, Cambridge Arts Theatre
7 December:	Ventnor, Isle of Wight, Winter Gardens
18 December:	London, Highbury Technical College
28 December:	Utrecht, Netherlands, Margriethal, Jaarbeurs. Paradise 2

1969

For the Lion and the Unicorn in the Forests of Faun Tour
Set List:
1 UNICORN/HOT ROD MOMMA
2 AFGHAN WOMAN
3 DEBORA

4 MUSTANG FORD
5 STACEY GROVE
6 SALAMANDA PALAGANDA
7 WIND QUARTETS
8 ONE INCH ROCK
9 CHARIOTS OF SILK
10 SEAL OF SEASONS
11 CONSUELA
12 NIJINSKY HIND
13 ONCE UPON THE SEAS OF ABYSSINIA
14 INTERSTELLAR OVERDRIVE
15 DO YOU REMEMBER
16 THE WIZARD

13 January: London, South Bank, Queen Elizabeth Hall.
               Two shows, at 6:15 p.m. and 9:00 p.m..
               Support for Vytas Serelis and David Bowie
25 January: Brondby, Denmark, Norregard Hallen,
               Brondby Pop Club
15 February: Birmingham, Town Hall
16 February: Croydon, Fairfield Hall
22 February: Manchester, Free Trade Hall
23 February: Bristol, Colston Hall
1 March: Liverpool, Philharmonic Hall
8 March: Brighton, Dome
11 April: London, Strand, Lyceum
12 May: Bath, Pavilion
17 May: Birmingham, Erdington, Mothers
31 May: Ryde, Isle of Wight, Ryde Pavilion,
               Cherokee's

14 June:	Bromley Technical College
27 June:	Sunderland, Whitburn, Bay Hotel

USA Tour

8 August:	San Francisco, Family Dog
9 August:	San Francisco, Family Dog
10 August:	San Francisco, Family Dog
11 August:	Los Angeles, Thee Experience
12 August:	Los Angeles, Thee Experience
13 August:	Los Angeles, Thee Experience
15 August:	New York, Greenwich Village, Café Au Go Go
16 August:	New York, Greenwich Village, Café Au Go Go
17 August:	New York, Greenwich Village, Café Au Go Go
18 August:	New York, Greenwich Village, Café Au Go Go
19 August:	New York, Greenwich Village, Café Au Go Go
20 August:	New York, Greenwich Village, Café Au Go Go
21 August:	New York, Greenwich Village, Café Au Go Go
22 August:	Chicago, Kinetic Playground
23 August:	Chicago, Kinetic Playground
30 August:	Prairieville, New Orleans Pop Festival
4 September:	Boston, The Boston Tea Party
5 September:	Boston, The Boston Tea Party
6 September:	Boston, The Boston Tea Party
9 September:	Philadelphia, Electric Factory
10 September:	Philadelphia, Electric Factory
11 September:	Philadelphia, Electric Factory
12 September:	Detroit, Grand Ballroom
13 September:	Detroit, Grand Ballroom
19 September:	Seattle, Eagles Auditorium
20 September:	Seattle, Eagles Auditorium

8 November: Leeds, Leeds University
21 November: Manchester, Free Trade Hall
22 November: Liverpool, Philharmonic Hall
28 November: Sunderland, Fillmore North, Locarno
29 November: Newcastle, City Hall
30 November: Birmingham, Erdington, Mothers
27 December: Croydon, Fairfield Hall

1970
21 January: Bournemouth, Winter Gardens
24 January: Plymouth, Devonport, Van Dyke Club
13 February: London, Strand, The Lyceum
8 February: Bridgend, The Kee Club
18 February: Brighton, The Dome
23 February: Dunstable, Civic Hall
14 March: Exeter, University of Exeter, Devonshire
                 House, Great Hall
29 March: Redcar, Coatham Hotel, Redcar Jazz Club
4 April: Cologne, Germany, Sporthalle, The
                 Progressive Pop Festival
6 April: Vienna, Austria, Konzerthaus
11 April: Dagenham, Village Roundhouse, The Blues
                 Club
21 April: London, Chalk Farm, Roundhouse. 1970
                 Pop Proms
9 May: London, Kensington, Imperial College
16 May: Nuremburg, Germany, Messehalle. Pop
                 Camp 70
17 May: Nuremburg, Germany, Messehalle. Pop
                 Camp 70

20 May:	Kirkcaldy, Adam Smith Hall
22 May:	Inverness, Empire Theatre
23 May:	Motherwell, Town Hall
24 May:	Dundee, Caird Hall
25 May:	Glasgow, Electric Garden
26 May:	Edinburgh, Usher Hall
30 May:	London, Kensington, Olympia Empire Hall
31 May:	Stoke-on-Trent, Gollum's Cave, Golden Torch Club
2 June:	Oxford, Town Hall
5 June:	Dudley, Castle Rock, Dudley Zoo
6 June:	Dunstable, Civic Hall
7 June:	Croydon, Greyhound
14 June:	Redcar, Coatham Hotel, Redcar Jazz Club
27 June:	Rotterdam, Netherlands, Kralingse Bos. The Holland Pop Festival
4 July:	Brentford, Brentford Football Ground, The Eyre
12 July:	Aachen, Germany, Reitstadion Soers. Aachen Open Air Pop Festival
22 August:	Copenhagen, Denmark, K B Hallen. The Copenhagen Beat Festival
30 August:	Redcar, Coatham Hotel, Redcar Jazz Club
6 September:	London, Chalk Farm, Roundhouse
11 September:	Edinburgh, Caley Cinema
12 September:	Dagenham, Village Roundhouse, The Blues Club
19 September:	Glastonbury. Pilton Pop Festival

T. Rex Tour

2 October:	London, Leytonstone, Red Lion
9 October:	Nottingham, Albert Hall
11 October:	Blackburn, King George's Hall
14 October:	Birmingham, Town Hall
15 October:	Sheffield, City Hall
20 October:	Southampton, Guildhall
25 October:	Essen, Germany, Grugahalle
29 October:	Dunstable, Civic Hall
30 October:	Hull, City Hall
31 October:	London, Kensington, Imperial College
4 November:	Liverpool, Mountford Hall
8 November:	Croydon, Greyhound
9 November:	Bristol, Colston Hall
12 November:	Oxford, Town Hall
24 November:	Guildford, Civic Hall
27 November:	Bournemouth, Winter Gardens
28 November:	Dagenham, Village Roundhouse, the Blues Club
3 December:	Glasgow, Green's Playhouse
4 December:	High Wycombe, Town Hall. The Students Union Christmas Ball
5 December:	Manchester, Manchester University, Main Debating Hall
6 December:	Corby, Civic Hall
7 December:	Wolverhampton, Civic Hall
11 December:	Welwyn Garden City, Community Centre
12 December:	Cardiff, Capitol Theatre
18 December:	Devizes, Box, Poporama
19 December:	Brighton, Regent Theatre, Big Apple

22 December: London, Chalk Farm, Roundhouse
31 December: Birmingham, Town Hall

1971

2 January: Sheffield, City Hall
3 January: Preston, Guildhall
4 January: Bradford, St George's Hall
7 January: Oxford, New Theatre
14 January: Liverpool, Empire Theatre
15 January: Stoke-on-Trent, Trentham Gardens
16 January: Aberystwyth, King's Hall
21 January: Southampton, Gaumont Theatre
25 January: London, Strand, The Lyceum
28 January: Paris, La Taverne de L'Olympia
4 February: Croydon, Fairfield Hall
6 February: London, University College
8 February: Cardiff, Top Rank
13 February: London, Barking, North East London
                 Polytechnic
14 February: Colchester, Essex University
15 February: Guildford, Civic Hall
16 February: Birmingham, Town Hall
17 February: Dundee, Caird Hall
20 February: Nottingham, Nottingham University
1 March: Cork, Ireland
2 March: Belfast, Northern Ireland
3 March: Dublin, Ireland
6 March: Reading, University of Reading
9 March: London, Playhouse Theatre
12 March: Bailrigg, University of Lancaster, Central Hall

| 19 March: | Coventry, Lanchester Polytechnic |
| 20 March: | Weston-super-Mare, Winter Gardens Pavilion |

USA Tour

9 April:	Detroit, Eastown Theatre
10 April:	Detroit, Eastown Theatre
12 April:	New York, Fillmore East Manhattan
13 April:	New York, Fillmore East Manhattan
14 April:	New York, Fillmore East Manhattan
15 April:	New York, Fillmore East Manhattan
19 April:	Los Angeles, Whisky a Go Go
20 April:	Los Angeles, Whisky a Go Go
21 April:	Quebec, Canada, Sarve Auditorium
23 April:	New York, Albany, State University of New York
24 April:	Arlington, Washington and Lee High School
25 April:	Philadelphia, The Spectrum Theater
30 April:	New York, Long Island, The Rock Pile
1 May:	New York, Long Island, The Rock Pile

1971 UK Tour
Set List:
1 ELEMENTAL CHILD
2 BELTANE WALK
3 JEWEL
4 ONE INCH ROCK
5 GIRL
6 DEBORA
7 RIDE A WHITE SWAN

8 HOT LOVE
9 GET IT ON
10 SUMMERTIME BLUES

9 May: Bournemouth, Winter Gardens
11 May: Portsmouth, Guildhall
14 May: Nottingham, Albert Hall
16 May: Manchester, Free Trade Hall
17 May: Sheffield, City Hall
19 May: Wolverhampton, Civic Hall
20 May: Newcastle, City Hall
21 May: Glasgow, Green's Playhouse
23 May: Croydon, Fairfield Hall
24 May: Bristol, Colston Hall
25 May: Leicester, De Montfort Hall
27 May: Bradford, St George's Hall
28 May: Liverpool, Philharmonic Hall
30 May: London, Chalk Farm, Roundhouse
26 June Amsterdam, Netherlands, Amsterdam Free Concert
2 July: Birmingham, Odeon
3 July: Boston, Lincolnshire, Starlight Rooms
9 July: London, Lewisham Odeon
17 July: Bath, The Pavilion
12 August: Bournemouth, Royal Ballrooms, Starker's Club
22 August: Stoke-on-Trent, Trentham Gardens
28 August: Rotherham, Clifton Park
29 August: Clacton-on-Sea, Weeley Festival
8 October: Rotterdam, Netherlands, Grote Zaal, De Doelen

9 October: Amsterdam, Netherlands, Concertgebouw

Autumn 1971 The Electric Warrior Tour
Set List:
1 CADILAC
2 BABY STRANGE
3 THUNDERWING
4 JEEPSTER
5 COSMIC DANCER
6 GIRL
7 SPACEBALL RICOCHET
8 DEBORA
9 RIDE A WHITE SWAN
10 HOT LOVE
11 GET IT ON
12 SUMMERTIME BLUES

19 October: Portsmouth, Guildhall
20 October: Plymouth, ABC
21 October: Cardiff, Capitol Theatre
23 October: Sheffield, City Hall
24 October: Croydon Fairfield Hall. Two shows
25 October: Bradford, St George's Hall
27 October: Brighton, The Dome
29 October: Glasgow, Green's Playhouse
30 October: Edinburgh, Empire Theatre
31 October: Newcastle, City Hall
4 November: Stockton-on-Tees, ABC
5 November: Birmingham, Town Hall
6 November: Manchester, Free Trade Hall

8 November:	Leicester, De Montfort Hall
9 November:	Lincoln, ABC
10 November:	Wigan, ABC
11 November:	Liverpool, Liverpool Stadium. Two shows

1972

15 January:	Boston, Lincolnshire, Gliderdrome, Starlight Club. Last gig of the Autumn 1971 Tour
28 January:	Oslo, Norway, Chateau Neuf
29 January:	Gothenburg, Sweden, Konserthuset
30 January:	Copenhagen, Denmark, Tivolis Koncertsal
31 January:	Hamburg, Germany, Grosser Saal, Musikhalle
1 February:	Münster, Germany, Halle Münsterland

USA Tour

15 February:	Hollywood, Hollywood Palladium
18 February:	Philadelphia, The Spectrum Theater
19 February:	Detroit, University of Detroit Memorial Hall
20 February:	Alexandria, Roller Rink
24 February:	Chicago, Auditorium
25 February:	Cleveland, Yorktown Theatre
27 February:	New York, Carnegie Hall

1972 UK Wembley and June Tour
Set List:
1 JEEPSTER
2 CADILLAC
3 BABY STRANGE
4 DEBORA

5 SPACEBALL RICOCHET
6 TELEGRAM SAM
7 METAL GURU
8 HOT LOVE
9 GET IT ON
10 SUMMERTIME BLUES

18 March:	London, Wembley Empire Pool. Two shows
9 June:	Birmingham, Odeon Two shows
10 June:	Cardiff, Capitol Theatre Two shows
16 June:	Manchester, Belle Vue
24 June:	Newcastle, City Hall Two shows

USA Tour

8 September:	Montreal, Canada, Pierre Fondes Arena
9 September:	Toronto, Canada, Massey Hall
12 September:	Boston, Massachusetts, The Orpheum/ Aquarius Theatre
14 September:	New York, Academy of Music. Two shows
16 September:	Passaic, New Jersey, Capitol Theatre
19 September:	Miami, Pirates World
20 September:	St Petersburg, Bayfront Center
22 September:	New Orleans, The Warehouse
23 September:	Atlanta, Municipal Auditorium
28 Sepatember:	Cleveland, Allen Theatre
29 September:	Detroit, Ford Auditorium
30 September:	Chicago, Auditorium Theatre
3 October:	St Louis, Kiel Auditorium
4 October:	Kansas City, Memorial Auditorium
5 October:	Oklahoma City, Civic Center Music Hall

6 October:	Shreveport, Louisiana, Civic Auditorium
7 October:	Houston, Music Hall
8 October:	Arlington, Texas, Texas Hall
13 October:	San Francisco, Winterland
14 October:	Santa Monica, Civic Auditorium
15 October:	Long Beach, California, Long Beach Auditorium

Far East Tour

28 November:	Tokyo, Japan, Budokan Hall
29 November:	Nagoya, Japan, Aichi-ken Taiikukan
1 December:	Osaka, Japan, Furitsu Taiikukan
4 December:	Tokyo, Japan, Budokan Hall
22 December:	London, Edmonton, Sundown
23 December:	London, Brixton, Sundown. Two shows

1973

13 February:	Berlin, Germany, Sportpalast
16 February:	Essen, Germany, Grugahalle
17 February:	Hamburg, Germany, Planten un Blomen, Halle 7
18 February:	Nuremburg, Germany, Neue Messehalle
19 February:	Vienna, Austria, Stadthalle Halle D
20 February:	Offenbach, Germany, Stadthalle
23 February:	Munich, Germany, Kongressaal Deutsches Museum
24 February:	Cologne, Germany, Sporthalle
12 March:	Paris, Olympia
15 March:	Gothenburg, Scandinavium
16 March:	Lund, Sweden, Olympen

17 March:	Aarhus, Denmark, Vejlby-Risskov Hallen
19 March:	Oslo, Norway, Chateau Neuf
21 March:	Copenhagen, Denmark, Frederiksberg, Falkoner Teatret
24 March:	Brussels, Belgium, National Vorst
10 April:	Watford, Town Hall. Marc made a guest appearance with ELO

USA Tour

20 July:	Milwaukee, Milwaukee Arena
21 July:	Chicago, Chicago Stadium
22 July:	Detroit, Cobo Hall
25 July:	Memphis, Mid-South Coliseum
28 July:	Tampa, Curtis Hixon Hall
29 July:	Atlanta, Omni
31 July:	Shreveport, Hirsch Auditorium
1 August:	Mobile, Mobile Municipal Auditorium
2 August:	Kansas City, Royal Stadium
3 August:	Baltimore, Civic Auditorium
4 August:	New York, Long Island, Uniondale, Nassau Coliseum
5 August:	Hartford, Dillon Stadium
10 August:	San Diego, Civic Theatre
11 August:	Santa Monica, Civic Auditorium
12 August:	Long Beach, Long Beach Auditorium
14 August:	Portland, Paramount Theatre
15 August:	Seattle, Paramount Northwest
16 August:	Vancouver, Pacific Exhibition Centre
17 August:	Salt Lake City, Salt Palace
18 August:	Denver, Denver Coliseum

19 August:	Lincoln, Nebraska, Pershing Auditorium
20 August:	Davenport, Quad City Stadium
21 August:	St Louis, Kiel Auditorium
23 August:	Binghamton, City Auditorium
24 August:	New Haven, New Haven Arena
25 August:	Harrisburg, State Farm Arena
26 August:	Boston, Boston Gardens
30 August:	Upper Darby, Tower Theatre
31 August:	Toronto, Canada, Canadian National Exhibition Grandstand
1 September:	Winnipeg, Canada, Winnipeg Arena
2 September:	Evansville, Roberts Municipal Stadium

Far East and Australia Tour

25 October:	Tokyo, Budokan Hall
27 October:	Nagoya, Ichirithu Taiikukan
28 October:	Osaka, Koseinenkin Hall
29 October:	Hiroshima, Yubin Chokin Hall
31 October:	Yahata, Shin-Nittetsu-Taiikukan
3 November:	Sydney, Hordern Pavilion
6 November:	Adelaide, Apollo Stadium
7 November:	Melbourne, Festival Hall
10 November:	Brisbane, Festival Hall

1974 Truck Off Tour
Set List:
1 20TH CENTURY BOY
2 CHARIOT CHOOGLE
3 TELEGRAM SAM
4 JEEPSTER

5 TEENAGE DREAM
6 THE GROOVER
7 BORN TO BOOGIE
8 METAL GURU
9 HOT LOVE
10 GET IT ON

21 January:	Newcastle, City Hall
22 January:	Glasgow, Apollo Theatre
24 January:	Sheffield, City Hall
26 January:	Manchester, Free Trade Hall
27 January:	Leicester, De Montfort Hall
28 January:	Birmingham, Odeon

USA Tour

26 September:	Upper Darby, Tower Theatre
27 September:	Worcester, Memorial Auditorium
28 September:	Johnstown, Ideal Park
29 September:	Columbus, Veterans Memorial Auditorium
2 October:	Parsippany, Joint in the Woods
5 October:	Clemson, Clemson University
8 October:	Long Beach, Long Beach Auditorium. Don Kirshner's Rock Show
11 October:	Fresno, Warner Theatre
14 October:	Phoenix, Show Palace
16 October:	Medford, Medford Arena
18 October:	Portland, Paramount Theatre
19 October:	Seattle, Paramount Northwest
20 October:	Victoria, Canada, Memorial Arena
21 October:	Vancouver, Pacific Coliseum

23 October:	Calgary, Stampede Corral
24 October:	Edmonton, Kinsmen Fieldhouse
26 October:	Winnipeg, University of Manitoba, Gymnasium
7 November:	St Louis, Kiel Opera House
8 November:	Chicago, Aragon Ballrooms
9 November:	Evansville, Roberts Municipal Stadium
11 November:	Cleveland, Agora Ballroom
13 November:	New Jersey, Elmwood Park, Mr D's
14 November:	Allentown, Rockne Hall
15 November:	Trenton, War Memorial Theatre
16 November:	Port Chester, Capitol Theatre
19 November:	Grand Rapids, Comstock Park, Thunder Chicken
20 November:	Lansing, Brewery
21 November:	Detroit, Michigan Palace
22 November:	Detroit, Michigan Palace

1975 Summer Tour
Set List:
1 JEEPSTER
2 20TH CENTURY BOY
3 TEENAGE DREAM
4 ZIP GUN BOOGIE
5 NEW YORK CITY
6 THE SOUL OF MY SUIT
7 HOT LOVE
8 GET IT ON

20 June:	Exeter, University of Exeter
13 July:	Douglas, Isle of Man, Palace Lido
23 July:	Great Yarmouth, Tiffany's
25 July:	Hastings, Pier Pavilion
26 July:	Folkestone, Leas Cliff Hall

1976 Futuristic Dragon Tour
Set List:
1 20TH CENTURY BOY
2 JEEPSTER
3 FUNKY LONDON CHILDHOOD
4 NEW YORK CITY
5 SOLID GOLD EASY ACTION
6 CHILDREN OF THE REVOLUTION
7 TEENAGE DREAM
8 TELEGRAM SAM
9 DEBORA
10 ONE INCH ROCK
11 RIDE A WHITE SWAN
12 DREAMY LADY
13 LONDON BOYS
14 HOT LOVE
15 GET IT ON

This was the standard set list, however the order did vary a little in the acoustic section (songs 9 to 12) 'Consuela' was definitely played at Sunderland's Empire Theatre.

Folkestone, Leas Cliff Hall: 'Ride a White Swan' omitted. Also, 'Debora' and 'One Inch Rock' were generally played as part of a medley.

5 February:	Chatham, Central Hall
6 February:	St Albans, City Hall
7 February:	Folkestone, Leas Cliff Hall
8 February:	Southend-on-Sea, Cliffs Pavilion
12 February:	Southport, Floral Hall
13 February:	Newark, Palace Theatre
14 February:	Withernsea, Grand Pavilion
15 February:	Sunderland, Empire Theatre
18 February:	London, The Lyceum, Strand
19 February:	Dunstable, Queensway Hall
20 February:	Bournemouth, Winter Gardens
23 February:	Birmingham, Town Hall
24 February:	Manchester, Free Trade Hall
28 February:	New Brighton, Winter Gardens, Floral Hall Pavilion
1 March:	Glasgow, Apollo Theatre
3 March:	Falkirk, Municipal Hall
4 March:	Motherwell, Concert Hall

1977 Dandy in the Underworld Tour
Set list:
1 JEEPSTER
2 VISIONS OF DOMINO
3 NEW YORK CITY
4 THE SOUL OF MY SUIT
5 GROOVE A LITTLE

6 TELEGRAM SAM
7 HANG-UPS
8 DEBORA
9 I LOVE TO BOOGIE
10 TEEN RIOT STRUCTURE
11 DANDY IN THE UNDERWORLD
12 HOT LOVE
13 GET IT ON

3 February:	Nantes, Club Macumba
4 February:	Bordeaux, Club Macumba
5 February:	Toulouse, Palais Des Sports
7 February:	Pau, Parc Beaumont
11 February:	Paris, Le Nashville
12 February:	Caen, Salle Omnisports, Troarn
10 March:	Newcastle, City Hall
11 March:	Manchester, Apollo Theatre
13 March:	Glasgow, Apollo Theatre
14 March:	Bristol, Colston Hall
17 March:	Birmingham, Odeon
18 March:	London, Rainbow Theatre
19 March:	West Runton, Pavilion
20 March:	Portsmouth, Locarno. Marc Bolan's last UK gig.
24 May:	Stockholm, Sweden, Gröna Lund. Marc Bolan's last live performance.

APPENDIX B
BIBLIOGRAPHY

Books

I would like to make special mention of the following books for anyone interested in learning even more about Marc Bolan – or the historical context in which he arose. These books have been invaluable sources of reference for me, and I hope you find these books and websites of as much interest as I have over the years:

A 1970s Teenager, by Simon Webb (The History Press, 2012)
Born to Boogie: The Songwriting of Marc Bolan, by Carl Ewens (Aureus Publishing, 2007)
Bolan: The Rise and Fall of a 20th Century Superstar, by Mark Paytress (Omnibus Press, 2002)
Britain in the 1970s an Annotated Timeline: The United

Kingdom and the Crisis in the 1970s, by John Mullen
(STAReBOOKS, 2016)

*Children of the Revolution: The Glam Rock Story 1970–
1975*, by Dave Thompson (Cherry Red Books, 2010)

Crisis? What Crisis? – Britain in the 1970s,
by Alwyn W. Turner (Aurum, 2013)

Marc Bolan: Born to Boogie, by Chris Welch and
Simon Napier-Bell (Plexus Publishing, 2008)

Marc Bolan: A Chronology, by Cliff McLenehan
(Helter Skelter Publishing, 2002)

Marc Bolan: A Tribute, by Ted Dicks and Paul Platz
(Springwood Books/Essex House, 1978)

Marc Bolan – The Legendary Years, John and Shan Bramley
(Smith Gryphon Ltd, 1992)

Marc Bolan – Natural Born Poet, Vol. 1, edited by John and
Shan Bramley (Bulletproof Cupid Publications, 2015)

Marc Bolan: Wilderness of the Mind, by John Willans and
Caron Thomas (Xanadu Publications, 1992)

Ride a White Swan: The Lives and Death of Marc Bolan,
by Lesley-Ann Jones (Hodder & Stoughton, 2012)

The Record Producers, by John Tobler and Stuart Grundy
(BBC, 1982)

*The Wizard's Gown – Rewoven: Beneath the Glitter of
Marc Bolan*, by Tony Stringfellow (Breeze Hayward
Publishing, 2007)

I have, where possible credited all the journalists and others I have referenced throughout *Beautiful Dreamer*. A great many reviews, articles and clippings are from personal scrapbook collections and many of these have simply been cut out. Like any teenager, when I cut out anything of interest on Marc Bolan, I rarely had the foresight to include the date or the writer! If I have omitted anyone while putting *Beautiful Dreamer* together then I apologise most sincerely. Those publications that I was able to pinpoint are:

Beat International
Disc and Music Echo
Melody Maker
National Rock Star
New Musical Express
Record Mirror
Sounds
The Times
ZigZag
Zoo World

Websites
www.rockbackpages.com
www.marcbolanmusic.com – Marc Bolan music – Unzipping the Abstract
www.tag.mercurymoon.co.uk
www.samgreen.co.uk/dandyintroduction – all about the 1977 Dandy in the Underworld Tour

ACKNOWLEDGEMENTS

My thanks to my publisher, John Blake, for his enthusiasm, faith and belief not just in this project, but in Marc Bolan as a twentieth-century icon. Steve Moon – I cannot do anything other than thank him unreservedly for his total dedication and encyclopaedic knowledge, coupled with his ability to get hold of anything research-wise that I needed (often at short notice). Steve also supplied many of the record and tour advertisements reproduced here and he kindly allowed me to reproduce his extensive list of all the tour dates (those that he is aware of, I must stress). To Tracey Addison for mopping his brow every time I messaged him or called him on the phone. To George Underwood for so readily agreeing to write about the story behind his creation of the sleeve artwork for the very first Tyrannosaurus Rex album *My People Were Fair* . . . John Wass (Rexpert extraordinaire) for stepping in at the eleventh hour with additional material from interviews with Herbie Flowers, Dino Dines and Tony Newman that took place some years ago.

To the hardcore Bolan fans I have had the pleasure to know for many more years than I (or they, no doubt) wish to recall, who supplied me with some wonderful memories from our teenage years following Marc: Val Slater, Colin Allen, Liz Marsden, Alistair Shield-Laignel, Michael Schnieders, Michael Green, Val Bolan Powell, Bari Watts and David Johnson. A special mention at this juncture to Mercedes Sullivan, who not only wrote but who also shared the diaries of her teenage years, which are still in her possession, and the contents therein. Kathleen Heron Andryszewski was one of the last of a small group of fans who saw and spoke to Marc Bolan just three days short of his sad death. She gave us permission to reproduce some of her pictures – taken on Tuesday, 13 September 1977 – even though many have been reproduced over the years with neither her permission nor her knowledge. Gary Nichol for some fantastic unpublished black-and-white images of Marc Bolan with girlfriend Gloria Jones and his son, Rolan. Gary also gave us access to some fabulous shots from the very last T. Rex gig in Sweden 1977. I am grateful to you all. I am indebted to the Mark Feld [a.k.a. Marc Bolan] Estate for – yet again – their cooperation and agreement to our use of lyrics, images and poetry under their copyright.

I would also like to mention another facet of keeping the Marc Bolan legacy strong: the tribute bands. Without doubt, the most consistent, durable and ever-present leading light of this movement is the group T. Rextasy. Over the decades there have been other bands, but this is the most authentic in the T. Rex mould. If you, like me, saw the original, you will already know what I refer to. If however, you never saw Marc Bolan and T. Rex, take a look when they are gigging. You will not be disappointed.

The second tribute band I'd like to acknowledge here is TooREX, who emerged comparatively recently. They are possibly slightly more polished, but they are still a bloody good night out when all you want to do is Bolan Boogie with friends and have a good time.

The third tribute band comes from a different angle. Beltane do not rely on a frontman with a vague or otherwise likeness to Marc Bolan. However, they bring an exciting alternative appreciation of the music of Marc Bolan by weaving the magic of acoustic and electric with a kick-ass percussionist.

Then again, you can always just listen to the original main man . . .

The following have encouraged, supported and made allowances for my 'drama queen' moments over the last two (only two?) years. All my Facebook friends – many I will never meet, but love you guys. My ex-work colleagues: Cath Brogan, Lee Wilson, Becky Kendall, Emma Newlove, Sam Thompson, Carole Bishop, Lynn Harper, Dee Parrish, Leslie Dawber, Karla Smith, Khadijah Khanum, David Fish, Angie Kokes and Kristine Wilkinson. My old friends George and Sally Rab. Alex and Dave Johnson, my wonderful, soon-to-be-wed niece Tez Johnson and her Gooner husband-to-be Wayne, and of course my fantastic wife Shan (and Scooby). If I have missed anyone else, please accept my apologies, as the mind is willing but my memory sometimes fails me.

The swirly curl of the Rumanian sun
limped from the gun of the sky
A caravan painted bold and a started
skull of Ivory ancestries,
the warehouse for the steep mountain wonderer
the gold man hidden in hides
a flapped torso tailored in urangatang tonge
a stout stick of mulberry
written on by the witch of song,
in her celestrial togo
and Saturn hourly fanned her
baked bones like an emporer
and a dailychild sang
tiny songs in the meadow by the faithstile
his groven ringlets filled with fogs,
his caplet of marigold shaped for conversation
with the outer world and his turn copper booties
deseined for wind walking

From the published 2015 collection of poetry,
Marc Bolan – Natural Born Poet